WANTED: A DIFFERENT THINKER

K. B. Roman

Kingdom Books

Published by Kingdom Books, an imprint of *CreativeJuicesBooks, Singapore (www.creativejuicesbooks.com)*

All Scripture quotations, unless otherwise indicated, are taken from *The Living Bible.* Copyright © 1971. Used by permission of Tyndale House Publishers, Inc., Carol Stream, Illinois 60188. All rights reserved.

Scripture quotations marked *NKJV* are taken from the *Holy Bible: New King James Version®*. Copyright © 1982 by Thomas Nelson. Used by permission. All rights reserved.

Scripture quotations marked *NIV* are taken from the *Holy Bible: New International Version®*. Copyright © 1973, 1978, 1984 International Bible Society. Used by permission of Zondervan Bible Publishers. All rights reserved.

Scripture quotations marked *NLT* are taken from the *Holy Bible, New Living Translation*, copyright © 1996, 2004, 2015 by Tyndale House Foundation. Used by permission of Tyndale House Publishers, Inc., Carol Stream, Illinois 60188. All rights reserved.

Scripture quotations marked *AMPC* are taken from the *Amplified® Bible, Classic Edition (AMPC)*, copyright © 1954, 1958, 1962, 1964, 1965, 1987 by The Lockman Foundation. Used by permission. www.Lockman.org

Scripture quotations marked *AMP* are taken from the *Amplified® Bible*, copyright © 1954, 1958, 1962, 1964, 1965, 1987 by The Lockman Foundation. Used by permission.

National Library Board, Singapore Cataloguing–in–Publication Data
Names: K. B. Roman.
Title: Wanted : a different thinker / K. B. Roman.
Description: Singapore : Kingdom Books, [2020]
Identifiers: OCN 1224298536 | ISBN 978-981-14-8970-9 (paperback)
Subjects: LCSH: Creative thinking--Religious aspects--Christianity. | Motivation (Psychology)--Religious aspects--Christianity.
Classification: DDC 248.4--dc23

Dedication page was designed using resources from Tartila.

Contents

To God Almighty, for inspiring this work and faithfully seeing it through to completion.

A Different Thinker

DO YOU HAVE WHAT IT TAKES TO BE A DIFFERENT THINKER? If so, you are just what this world needs… because everyone is looking for that one person who can think and do things differently; who can come up with unusual and uncommon ways to achieve unusual and uncommon results.

The world is going through one crisis after another, with people everywhere waking up each day to fear, misery and despair. Many lack genuine peace, joy, hope and fulfilment in their lives. They are looking for keys to the locked doors they have been trying to open for the longest time. They are looking for someone to help them solve the perplexities of life: to show them this one particular open door that will lead to other open doors; to assist them in the discovery of their true identity and purpose.

A different thinker is needed. Someone who can look at situations from a fresh angle; who can explore and exhaust every possibility; who can solve problems creatively and excellently. Someone who consistently lives above the limitations that have constrained everyone else.

The world is full of people who are satisfied with just getting by with average results. But once in a while—not often—you will find mavericks who are tired of mediocrity, of seeing everyone around them doing the same old things and getting the same old run-of-the-mill results. These are the independent thinkers who want to avoid all of that—all the common, limited ways of thinking and doing things.

A different thinker is born each time someone is tired of the old, unproductive ways of thinking and doing things; each time an individual stops trying to be a carbon copy of everyone else; each time you and I decide, courageously and unapologetically, to explore and develop our own originality and unique qualities.

Change is needed, but that change will not just occur by itself. You need someone to make it happen; the solution for what troubles humanity lies in the hands of humanity. You and I can be the hands the Creator uses to help those in need. You and I can be the change the world needs. You and I can decide to think and do things differently.

People will not want to change themselves or the way they do things *until they see the need for change.* They will not see the need for change until they know and understand what the real problems are. They won't easily see those problems—and the solutions for them—unless they are able to think differently. They won't be able to think differently until they can see and understand their world differently. They can't see and understand their world differently until they themselves decide to do so. In short, people can't think differently until they *choose* to do so. You have to make this choice yourself; it all starts with *your* decision.

My prayer is that, as you read this book, you will be inspired and encouraged to step out of your comfort zone and make that decision. To help you make an informed choice, I will be discussing what it takes to be a different thinker and how it is possible for you to become one. As we journey through the following pages, we will also be looking at various independent thinkers who have been movers and shakers in their time. We will examine their characters and unique qualities from the viewpoint of God's Word.

Throughout this book, we will be taking God's Word as our standard—because it *is* the standard for our lives. Everything flows from the Word of God; it alone has the power to transform every one of us into a different thinker. The Bible tells us that all things are possible with God and with those who believe (*Matthew 17:20, 19:26; Luke 1:37; Mark 10:27; Jeremiah 32: 17, 27*).

Man is the most powerful creature God has created to live on this earth. We have been made in God's image (*Genesis 1:26-27; John 10:34*). We can think of anything and achieve it. This has been proven to be true by many godly men and women whose stories can be found in the Bible. They did great exploits for God and made history because of different thinking. We will be discussing some of their achievements in the following chapters of this book.

When man has exhausted every recourse and reached rock bottom, the only hope that remains is the Word of God. God's Word is alive and powerful; it alone has the power to bring non-existent things into existence—the same way all of creation was spoken into existence by God. The Word of God is always reliable and relevant. It says what it means and means what it says. The Bible is the only book that has stood the test of time and still does. This is why we are taking God's Word as the foundation on which you and I can build and expand our capacity to think independently.

Let us begin now.

CHAPTER 1

Believes the Possibility of the Impossible

A DIFFERENT THINKER IS ABLE TO BELIEVE THE IMPOSSIBLE. If you want to be a different thinker, you have to start to believe that the impossible *can* become possible. A different thinker knows that there are always options in life: that we *do* have a choice, in whatever situation we are in, to decide what we want from that situation.

The truth is that you *can* make a choice to get the possible out of the impossible; you *can* determine the kind of results you want; you *do* have the power to transform situations and get what you want from them. All of this is possible, but only on one condition: *that you give God His rightful position in your life.*

To be a different thinker, you have to place God *in the centre of your life.* You have to put your faith and trust fully in Him. It is *only when you fully believe in the God of the impossible* that you are able to believe the possibility of the impossible and to know beyond a doubt that your God can make something out of nothing. Start looking at the creation that God spoke into existence and get encouraged to follow in the footsteps of your Maker.

How to have absolute faith and trust in God

What does it mean to have absolute faith and trust in God? It means you have no doubts at all, but you believe fully in God's power and ability. It means you have learnt to leave everything that concerns you in the hands and care of God.

It means that you do not burden yourself with unnecessary worries or anxieties. You see and expect possibility after taking your problems to God. You fully believe that God says what He means and means what He says in His Word. You are very sure, *beyond all doubt*, of God's faithfulness: that God is a covenant-keeping God, a promise-keeping God, and that you will get what God promised you in His Word.

To be a different thinker means trusting God to bring to fulfilment what He has promised. It means that your life is determined, defined and clear, because you *know* your God. Like Job, you can say with confidence, "I know that my Redeemer lives" (*Job 19:25*). Like Paul, you can say, "I know the one in whom I trust" (*2 Timothy 1:12*). It means that you believe God is able to do exceedingly abundantly above all that you ask or think (*Ephesians 3:20*).

To be a different thinker means to trust that God knows best. It means that you trust God for the best answers and solutions. Even when you haven't received any answer for the longest time, you continue to trust that He is busy working out all things for your good. You know that those who endure to the end will be saved. You are not put down, put out, or put off when the things you want are not happening, the way you want, at the time you want.

To be a different thinker is to be immovable, focused, resolute: no second thought, no backup plan, no other option for you. You are single-minded about God. Sitting on the fence is not your thing. No place for you in the middle of the road either. You are able to stand your ground, like the three Hebrew men who said to the king, "Our God whom we serve is able to deliver us from the burning fiery furnace, and He will deliver us from your hand, O king" (*Daniel 3:17, NKJV*).

To be a different thinker, you have to learn to dig in your heels in the face of challenges. Make the immovable Word of God your foundation, and you will not be moved or forced to retreat. You will be unbowed even in the worst of situations, because you have this incredible faith in God. You will understand that the darker the night, the brighter will be the day; that, no matter how dark it gets, the night will not last forever. Daybreak will come, and the sun will shine again—because there is a season for everything.

A different thinker understands that some things need to be destroyed to be made new, to be scattered so that they can be assembled in new ways; that rest and peace come after the fiercest storm; that weeping may endure for a night, but joy always comes in the morning. This knowledge enables him[1] to live a joyful life even in the midst of challenges. It enables him to live each day with hope in God, because he knows he will not be put to shame for doing so.

Different thinking enables you to see that what looks like the end of all things may signal the beginning of new things: that the highest mountain can be levelled down, the lowest valley exalted high, the crooked way made straight, so that God's power and glory may be revealed. Such insight empowers you to persist in doing what needs to be done, patiently and faithfully—even when the situation stays unchanged, gets worse, or turns against you in unexpected ways. It drives you to continue working as if everything depends on you. It is why you are able to do what you do as a service to the Lord, knowing your labor in God is not in vain. People may not appreciate what you do, but you know God sees and He won't forget what you are doing for Him.

---

[1] Throughout this book, all references to the different thinker as "he", "him" or "his" should be read as inclusive of the female gender too.

Circumstances may look bleak now, but you know that in due season you will reap the harvest. When the time is right, you will come back rejoicing with your reward. You won't allow yourself to be bothered about negative "facts and realities" or what seems to be the "horrible truth", because you have Someone who is the Way, the Truth and the Life. Someone who is in control of everything. Someone more powerful, authoritative and influential than your situation.

Once you have involved the God of all creation in your situation, you need to forge ahead with whatever you have to do. Do not be put off by unfavorable conditions; do not be paralyzed into inaction. Remember: "He who observes the wind [and waits for all conditions to be favorable] will not sow, and he who regards the clouds will not reap" (*Ecclesiastes 11:4, AMPC*).

The man who locked up the heavens

The prophet Elijah was a different thinker who had power and authority over kings, queens, kingdoms and situations:

> Then Elijah said to Ahab, "Go and enjoy a good meal! For I hear a mighty rainstorm coming!"
>
> So Ahab prepared a feast. But Elijah climbed to the top of Mount Carmel and got down on his knees, with his face between his knees, and said to his servant, "Go and look out toward the sea."
>
> He did, but returned to Elijah and told him, "I didn't see anything."
>
> Then Elijah told him, "Go again, and again, and again, seven times!"
>
> Finally, the seventh time, his servant told him, "I saw a little cloud about the size of a man's hand rising from the sea."

Then Elijah shouted, "Hurry to Ahab and tell him to get into his chariot and get down the mountain, or he'll be stopped by the rain!"

And sure enough, the sky was soon black with clouds, and a heavy wind brought a terrific rainstorm. Ahab left hastily for Jezreel, and the Lord gave special strength to Elijah so that he was able to run ahead of Ahab's chariot to the entrance of the city!

1 Kings 18:41-46

Elijah understood what God had said in His Word: "You are gods [since you judge on My behalf, as My representatives]" (*Psalm 82:6, AMPC*). He understood that he was representing God in the world. So, as God's ambassador, he took things upon himself; he acted on behalf of God.

He wasn't looking down on himself. He wasn't taking his calling lightly. He wasn't about to disappoint his Master. He was fully cognizant of the power, authority and control bestowed upon him as an ambassador of the highest of kingdoms. He understood the advantages and privileges that came with being an ambassador of the kingdom of God.

We too are ambassadors of Christ. God's Word tells us that "as He is, so are we in this world" (*1 John 4:17, AMPC*). When God makes us His representatives, He doesn't take over what should be our part. He has made man to dominate, rule and reign on earth (*Genesis 1:26-28*). That was why, when God thought that the drought had gone on long enough, He consulted Elijah on the issue.

God is not a trespasser or dictator. He is not nosey. He wouldn't have just brought down the rain, when He wasn't the one who had stopped it in the first place! That wouldn't have been right. It was Elijah who had stopped the rain.

> Then Elijah the prophet… told King Ahab, "As surely as the Lord God of Israel lives—the God whom I worship and serve—there won't be any dew or rain for several years until I say the word!"
>
> *1 Kings 17:1*

It was Elijah—not God—who gave the word to stop the rain. So, it was up to Elijah to give the word to bring back the rain. It is up to us to give the word in every situation. For God to act on earth, He needs our permission and cooperation. *He wants to work with us.* He wants us to tell Him what we want to see happening in the world, and He will honor that. He is waiting for us to contact Him for something to be done on earth. This is what we call prayer: communicating and consulting with God about what is going on in the world He gave to us.

Not that He won't continue to do His best for humanity —even if no one is prepared to ask Him to do it. He will always reach out to help us. He is faithful. His plans and purposes for us have not changed. He still loves us with the same love He had when He first created man—even when we continuously disappoint Him, committing the most heinous sins imaginable and constantly coming up with new, advanced ways of wickedness. But God has not dealt with us according to our sins nor punished us according to our iniquities (*Psalm 103:10*).

Even when no one is reaching out to God to ask for His help, He is able to raise up an intercessor for humanity. He can put a burden on a man, He can fill a woman with passion, so that these ambassadors of His may represent Him on earth and present to Him the challenges we are facing in our time—so that He can come to our rescue.

Whatever calamity is happening on earth, we need to understand that God is not to be blamed for it. When things are not going well in the world, He is not to be blamed. He is waiting for us to do what we are meant to do. We are the ones in charge of the earth—with His help. God is in charge of heaven. He has handed over earth, the work of His hands, to man. Because of this, there is no way He can do anything in the world without working together with man. He has set limits on Himself when it comes to ruling this planet:

> God said, Let Us [Father, Son, and Holy Spirit] make mankind in Our image, after Our likeness, and let them have **complete authority** over the fish of the sea, the birds of the air, the [tame] beasts, and over all of the earth, and over everything that creeps upon the earth.
>
> So God created man in His own image, in the image and likeness of God He created him; male and female He created them.
>
> And God blessed them and said to them, Be fruitful, multiply, and fill the earth, and subdue it [using all its vast resources in the service of God and man]; and have **dominion** over the fish of the sea, the birds of the air, and over every living creature that moves upon the earth.
>
> *Genesis 1:26-28, AMPC*

We were made to rule and reign over the earth. This is the reason God made us in His image and after His likeness. This is the kind of power, the level of authority we have over everything on earth—so much so that God Himself has to consult us before He can do anything. In Elijah's case, God saw the need for rain, and He consulted and discussed the issue with the person who had stopped the rain. God is a God of order; He respects positions and principles.

Elijah understood the kind of power and authority he had as a representative of God in the world. This man was able to lock up the heavens so that not a drop of rain fell for three and a half years. He went away with the keys, and no one else had a duplicate set. And he didn't even pray to God to stop the rain. He simply declared to King Ahab: "There won't be any rain for the next several years until I say so." *Now, that's real power and authority!*

Now, King Ahab was a man who had sold himself utterly to wickedness. To make matters worse, he had married an evil woman, Jezebel. So, Elijah had the sins of this king, his queen, and the people up to his neck. That was why he stopped the rain: to punish them for their wickedness. But there came a time when he had to bring the rain back. He had to bring back what he had taken away.

So, Elijah told the king, "Go and have a good meal, for I hear a mighty rainstorm coming!" He said this even before there was any physical sound or sight of rain—not even the tiniest raincloud! Only a different thinker could have said such a thing. His status as a major prophet of God was at stake: he *had* to unlock what he had locked up. This was the reason he refused to accept the answer his servant gave him six times, that there was no sign of rain. This was why he persisted until his servant finally brought him the only answer he wanted to hear.

He wanted to hear the sound of the mighty rainstorm that he had told the king about. He wasn't about to settle for less than what he had seen and heard in his spirit. He was immovable and unstoppable in what he wanted to achieve: to see, in the physical, the manifestation of what he saw in his spirit. He wanted to see the rainclouds. That was all this man wanted. Nothing else.

He sent his servant to look at the skies. The man went six times, and each time he came back with a negative report: there were no clouds at all. But Elijah believed the clouds should be there. His mind was focused on one thing—rain. He would not accept any other answer. He sent the man back six times because he wasn't going to waver from what he believed. The seventh time, the servant finally came back with the only answer the man of God wanted to hear.

Elijah could think out of the ordinary, and that was how he got extraordinary results. An ordinary thinker would have given up at the first, second or third sign of failure; he wouldn't have gone all the way to see the matter through. Most of us give up too soon. We expend all our time and effort, only to throw in the towel when we are almost on the point of a breakthrough.

We say, "I'm so tired, I can't take it anymore." We forget we may be feeling this tired because we have come a long way, but we are about to reach our goal! We give up because we believe it's all been for nothing. This is not how a different thinker thinks. He will see a way through, where many—having come to a roadblock—would have retraced their steps. He will still be holding on where others have let go. He will still be pursuing where others have turned back.

If you want to be a different thinker, you have to be prepared to throw out old ways that haven't worked well for you and aren't taking you anywhere. You have to decide to change gears, to leave the natural realm and get into the supernatural. When you see "realities and facts" of impossibilities everywhere, you have to tell yourself that it is time to stop walking by sight and start walking by faith; it is time to call the things that are not there as though they are (*Romans 4:17*).

A different thinker's faith acts as a vehicle that carries him wherever he wants to go. This was indeed true of Elijah: he "climbed to the top of Mount Carmel and got down on his knees, with his face between his knees" (*1 Kings 18:42*). He wouldn't have put his face between his knees for nothing. It was a serious moment. He expected results to come out of what he did—and he got them.

Elijah got what he wanted because he believed and trusted his God, who had promised to send the rain. He had already believed the positive report of the Lord long before he received the negative reports of his servant. There was no place for those contrary reports because he was fully occupied with the main report from his God. The promises of God took precedence over all he saw in the natural realm. Physical facts, realities, feelings and emotions can never change the truth of God's Word.

If you want to be a different thinker, you have to live your life in God. This is not the kind of lifestyle where you visit with God as and when circumstances and time permit. It is a lifelong commitment. It is to be lived and applied in all situations and areas of your life. You have to live and walk by faith; you have to understand that, without faith, you cannot please God. You have to allow yourself to be led by the Spirit, so that you can fulfil God's purposes and find meaning and fulfilment in life.

Take God at His Word—literally

"So now, brethren, I commend you to God and to the word of His grace, which is able to build you up and give you an inheritance among all those who are sanctified."

Acts 20:32, NKJV

Start taking God's Word seriously. Treasure and respect His Word, and believe fully in it. Do not doubt at all. A different thinker sees God's Word as the first, the last, and the only solution to every problem. He takes it as the only standard and authority in his life. Because he believes fully in its power, he can stand his ground, firm and unshakeable in the midst of the fiercest storm.

A different thinker knows how to prompt God to action using His Word—how to hold God to His Word and to the promises in it. If you want to be a different thinker, you have to go beyond just believing in the Word: you have to take one step further and *act on the Word.* You have to start operating on the written and revealed Word of God, the Bible. Start trusting in the faithfulness of God's Word. Understand that not a single word of His Word will ever go unfulfilled. In so doing, you will be able to wait with joy, hope, peace, assurance, strength and grace, while God works out His solution for you.

A different thinker understands the important role that God's Word plays in developing his faith. The Bible tells us that "you can never please God without faith, without depending on him" (*Hebrews 11:6*). This faith that pleases God comes through, by, from and with the Word of God. It is a faith that is inspired, ignited, fueled, encouraged and grown by the Word (*Romans 10:17*). The Word is the beginning and foundation of faith.

Faith comes from knowing and understanding God's Word. Your faith is strengthened by and in the Word of God. It is established, developed, grounded and grown in the Word. It thrives on the Word of God. It comes from spending quality time in the Word: reading the Word, listening to it, and meditating on it with the help of the Holy Spirit.

A different thinker builds and strengthens his faith through good practices: he confesses and speaks the Word of God into every situation; he prays the Word, and he also prays *with* the Word. He fills his whole being with the Word. He allows the Word to saturate and dominate him:

> You, through Your commandments, make me wiser than my enemies, for [Your words] are ever before me.
>
> I have better understanding and deeper insight than all my teachers, because Your testimonies are my meditation.
>
> I understand more than the aged, because I keep Your precepts [hearing, receiving, loving, and obeying them] ... Through Your precepts I get understanding; therefore I hate every false way.
>
> *Psalm 119:98-100, 104, AMPC*

You need to stand in, on, by, with, and for the Word. Start to encourage yourself in the Word and constantly meditate on it. Meditate on its benefits; think of what is at stake if you don't have the Word in you, the way you should be having it. Allow the Holy Spirit to help you in all areas of your life. Ignite your faith by living your life in the Spirit. This is the lifestyle of a different thinker.

Marching to the beat of a different drummer

Because of his knowledge and understanding of God and His Word, a different thinker believes that the difficult can be made easy or less difficult. Many things in life are regarded as difficult or impossible. But we know that the people who have changed, made or directed history are the ones who never regard anything as impossible to achieve.

When everyone says, "I can't do this or that because it is difficult, if not impossible," the different thinker speaks a different language. He says, "It may be so or seem so, but I *can* do it. It may be hard, but it is not impossible. It may be impossible to others, but it's not so to me. It may never have been done before, but that doesn't mean it can't be done at all." *And he goes for it!*

When people tell you, "This is impossible because it hasn't been done before," say to them, "That may be so, but I will be the first to do it!" To be a different thinker, you have to start thinking like an initiator, an originator, an inventor; you have to have the mindset of a pioneer and creator. Start to think for yourself. Don't just follow the crowd blindly, but learn to trust in your own ability to make wise judgments and decisions. With this mindset, you will become recognized as a leader—because you are able to see a way where others see only impossibilities and difficulties; you are able to find a way out that wasn't there before.

A different thinker is not only for the open, broad road. He has the discipline to trek through narrow, difficult paths too. He understands that there is everything to be gained in persevering and enduring to the end. Giving up easily isn't his thing. This attitude makes him stand out from the crowd. What causes others to lose hope and faith only spurs him to press on; what causes everyone else to give up only brings out a rare courage and strength within him, and a resolve to carry out his mission to completion.

When everyone around you is moaning about how bad the situation looks, don't join in the chorus. Say instead, "Things are looking good!" When people are talking about how hard life is, turn around and tell them, "Life is great!"

Say this, not because life is already great or things are looking good for you, but because you are walking by faith and not by sight. Say it because you know that there is power in speaking things into existence. Say it because you understand that the world and all that is in it were spoken into existence by God—and since you have been made in the image and likeness of God, you can do the same.

A different thinker is not moved by difficulties but he moves them. He is not shaken by challenges but he shakes them. He is not easily influenced, changed or directed by his circumstances, but he influences, changes and directs those circumstances. He has learnt to dominate and triumph over every situation that was meant to dominate and defeat him.

You are not meant to be a victim but a victor over circumstances. Do not be troubled about your situation, but trouble that situation until it bows down to you. Do not dance to the tune of your enemy the devil, by giving in to discouragement, but take courage in the fact that all things work together for good to those who love God, to those who are called according to His purpose (*Romans 8:28*).

Bootlickers end up getting the boot

When Nebuchadnezzar was king of Babylon, he ordered everyone in his kingdom to bow down before a huge golden image he had set up. Anyone who did not worship it would be thrown into his fiery furnace. As all the people fell down before this golden idol, they saw a strange sight —three men who were not obeying the king's command.

Those three men—Shadrach, Meshach and Abednego— were different thinkers. They would not follow the crowd. They obeyed God rather than man—the God who had commanded, "You shall not make yourselves any idols...

You must never bow or worship it in any way" (*Exodus 20:4*). They refused to be intimidated just because everyone else feared to disobey the king. They dug in their heels deeper and stood their ground.

> But some officials went to the king and accused some of the Jews of refusing to worship!
>
> "Your Majesty," they said to him, "you made a law that everyone must fall down and worship the gold statue… and that anyone who refuses will be thrown into a flaming furnace. But there are some Jews out there—Shadrach, Meshach, and Abednego… who have defied you, refusing to serve your gods or to worship the gold statue you set up."
>
> *Daniel 3: 8-12*

In other words, their accusers were saying this to the king: "There are different thinkers among us. They have decided to do a different thing, when you have commanded everyone to do the same thing. They are doing things differently from how everyone else is doing them."

Those three men did things differently, and that was why they stood out from the crowd. They were not afraid to differ from everyone else. They were not afraid to reveal that they were of a different point of view. They were not afraid to stand firm to the end. When they were warned about the terrible punishment they would get for their disobedience, this was what they said to the king:

> "O Nebuchadnezzar, we are not worried about what will happen to us. If we are thrown into the flaming furnace, our God is able to deliver us; and he will deliver us out of your hand, Your Majesty.

"But if he doesn't, please understand, sir, that even then we will never under any circumstance serve your gods or worship the gold statue you have erected."

Daniel 3: 16-18

Nobody had ever answered the king so boldly before! This was an extraordinary case that had to be dealt with in an extraordinary way:

Then Nebuchadnezzar was filled with fury and his face became dark with anger at Shadrach, Meshach, and Abednego. He commanded that the furnace be heated up seven times hotter than usual, and called for some of the strongest men of his army to bind Shadrach, Meshach, and Abednego, and throw them into the fire.

Daniel 3: 19-20

Those three Jews were thrown into a furnace seven times hotter than usual. It wasn't always that hot but, because the king was dealing with different thinkers, he had to apply different laws. When those three noticed that a different law was being applied to their case, they stuck to being different. And God was faithful to deliver them, because those who put their faith in Him will never be disappointed.

But suddenly, as he was watching, Nebuchadnezzar jumped up in amazement and exclaimed to his advisors, "Didn't we throw three men into the furnace?"

"Yes," they said, "we did indeed, Your Majesty."

"Well, look!" Nebuchadnezzar shouted. "I see *four* men, unbound, walking around in the fire, and they aren't even hurt by the flames! And the fourth looks like a god!"

Daniel 3: 24-25

What those three guys had done was to prepare a platform for God to act and show Himself strong on their behalf. This was such a fiery furnace that flames were leaping out of it and killing the king's strongest soldiers, even as they threw the three Jews in (*Daniel 3: 23*). Yet those three men simply got up and started walking around in the furnace with not a single burn on them. And a fourth man—the Lord Himself—appeared and joined them in their walk!

Those three Jews experienced the supernatural power of God because they were different thinkers. They were not following the crowd but their God. And, because they obeyed God rather than man, they were promoted to greatness by the same king who had thrown them into the fire:

> Then Nebuchadnezzar came as close as he could to the open door of the flaming furnace and yelled: "Shadrach, Meshach, and Abednego, servants of the Most High God! Come out! Come here!" So they stepped out of the fire.
>
> Then the princes, governors, captains, and counselors crowded around them and saw that the fire hadn't touched them—not a hair of their heads was singed; their coats were unscorched, and they didn't even smell of smoke!
>
> Then Nebuchadnezzar said, "Blessed be the God of Shadrach, Meshach, and Abednego, for he sent his angel to deliver his trusting servants when they defied the king's commandment and were willing to die rather than serve or worship any god except their own. Therefore, I make this decree, that any person of any nation, language, or religion who speaks a word against the God of Shadrach, Meshach, and Abednego shall be torn limb from limb and his house knocked into a heap of rubble. For no other God can do what this one does."

Then the king gave promotions to Shadrach, Meshach, and Abednego, so that they prospered greatly there in the province of Babylon.

Daniel 3: 26-30

The common belief is that only the bootlickers get the good things in life. But staying true to your convictions does have a way of paying off; often handsomely too. Extraordinary choices have a way of birthing extraordinary results. Those men dared to be different, to raise up the banner of the Lord —and, for that, God had no other option but to reward them.

Now, you may be asking: who were those men, and what made them so different? The Bible tells us they were captives that the Babylonian king had brought back from Jerusalem:

Then he ordered Ashpenaz, who was in charge of his palace personnel, to select some of the Jewish youths brought back as captives—young men of the royal family and nobility of Judah—and to teach them the Chaldean language and literature.

"Pick strong, healthy, good-looking lads," he said; "those who have read widely in many fields, are well informed, alert and sensible, and have enough poise to look good around the palace."

The king assigned them the best of food and wine… during their three-year training period, planning to make them his counselors when they graduated. Daniel, Hananiah, Mishael, and Azariah were four of the young men chosen… However, their superintendent gave them Babylonian names, as follows: Daniel was called Belteshazzar; Hananiah was called Shadrach; Mishael was called Meshach; Azariah was called Abednego.

Daniel 1: 3-7

There were four men who stood out, three of whom we have already met: Shadrach, Meshach and Abednego (who were also called Hananiah, Mishael and Azariah). In the following pages, we will turn our attention to the fourth: Daniel, a man so outstanding that he became, in time, ruler over the whole of Babylon—with his three friends as his assistants—and chief over the king's wise men (*Daniel 2:48*).

Those four youths were the best of the best: able-bodied, handsome, well-read, smart young men from the Jewish nobility, who could conduct themselves with aplomb in the king's court. Handpicked from among many other candidates, they were given the best royal education and, upon graduation, promoted to be the king's counselors. Above every quality and qualification that they possessed, they loved and served their God faithfully.

> God gave these four youths great ability to learn, and they soon mastered all the literature and science of the time; and God gave to Daniel special ability in understanding the meanings of dreams and visions.
>
> When the three-year training period was completed, the superintendent brought all the young men to the king for oral exams, as he had been ordered to do. King Nebuchadnezzar had long talks with each of them, and none of them impressed him as much as Daniel, Hananiah, Mishael, and Azariah. So they were put on his regular staff of advisors.
>
> And in all matters requiring information and balanced judgment, the king found these young men's advice ten times better than that of all the skilled magicians and wise astrologers in his realm.
>
> *Daniel 1: 17-20*

The true mark of a different thinker

Daniel was highly regarded by four successive kings: Nebuchadnezzar and, after him, Belshazzar, followed by Darius and, thereafter, Cyrus. There was something special about Daniel that gained him favor with every one of those kings. This of course made the other officials jealous, and so, they sought to discredit him. But they couldn't find any fault in him, because he was excellent in every way.

> Daniel soon proved himself more capable than all the other presidents and governors, for he had great ability, and the king began to think of placing him over the entire empire as his administrative officer.
>
> This made the other presidents and governors very jealous, and they began searching for some fault in the way Daniel was handling his affairs so that they could complain to the king about him. But they couldn't find anything to criticize! He was faithful and honest and made no mistakes. So they concluded, "Our only chance is his religion!"
>
> *Daniel 6: 3-5*

He was a cut above them, so much so that there was nothing they could do to him! Their only chance lay in finding fault with the commands of his God. *Now, that's always a very dangerous thing to do!* But—fools that they were—they went ahead and set their trap. They said to the king:

> "May King Darius live forever! The royal administrators, prefects, satraps, advisers and governors have all agreed that the king should issue an edict and enforce the decree that anyone who prays to any god or human being during the next thirty days, except to you, Your Majesty, shall be thrown into the lions' den.

"Now, Your Majesty, issue the decree and put it in writing so that it cannot be altered—in accordance with the law of the Medes and Persians, which cannot be repealed." So King Darius put the decree in writing.

Daniel 6: 6-9, NIV

They knew that Daniel prayed daily to his God; so, they got the king to pass a law prohibiting anyone from doing just that. This was a law that benefited no one; it was enacted for the sole purpose of destroying one man in particular—Daniel. But Daniel wasn't intimidated. He continued to pray to God as he had always done, and he did it openly.

He had to decide who his real master was—the God of all creation or the king of Babylon. He wasn't going to let others force their point of view on him. He was an independent thinker. He wasn't going to be a bootlicker, just for the sake of the privileges that came with obeying the king. He wasn't going to be afraid of the one king, when he had the support and backup of the Most High, the King of kings.

Different thinking had made him a very important, popular and famous man—so much so that his enemies wanted at all cost to eliminate him. His faithfulness exposed their corrupt dealings, and that was why they wanted to do away with him. They couldn't take the standard of discipline he demanded of them as their leader. They couldn't get used to his demands for honesty and transparency, and for responsibility and accountability in the workplace.

This man was a threat to them because of the spirit of excellence in him. He demanded from them the kind of loyalty they couldn't give. He wanted things to be done correctly and in an orderly manner. He wanted the right things to be done the right way and for the right reasons.

He wanted things to be done at the right time. He wanted everything to be done in an excellent manner, to achieve excellent results. He wanted things to be done exceptionally to achieve exceptional results. He was determined to reach the end of all perfection in all he did, and he therefore expected those working with him and under him to do the same. Many were not ready to do all that.

> Then the men thronged to Daniel's house and found him praying there, asking favors of his God. They rushed back to the king and reminded him about his law. "Haven't you signed a decree," they demanded, "that permits no petitions to any God or man—except you…? And anyone disobeying will be thrown to the lions?"
>
> "Yes," the king replied, "it is 'a law of the Medes and Persians,' that cannot be altered or revoked."
>
> *Daniel 6: 11-12*

They wanted to punish him for thinking he was smarter than them. The conflict between them started because of different thinking. They wanted to see what would come out of his different thinking when he was exposed to serious challenges. But Daniel displayed the true mark of a different thinker: he stood firm in what he believed to the end. He maintained his composure. He didn't panic in the face of challenges. He took control of the situation and didn't allow the situation to take control of him.

> In the evening the men went together to the king and said, "Your Majesty, you know that according to the law of the Medes and the Persians, no law that the king signs can be changed." So at last the king gave orders for Daniel to be arrested and thrown into the den of lions…

Very early the next morning, the king got up and hurried out to the lions' den. When he got there, he called out in anguish, "Daniel, servant of the living God! Was your God, whom you serve so faithfully, able to rescue you from the lions?"

Daniel answered, "Long live the king! My God sent his angel to shut the lions' mouths so that they would not hurt me, for I have been found innocent in his sight. And I have not wronged you, Your Majesty."

The king was overjoyed and ordered that Daniel be lifted from the den. Not a scratch was found on him, for he had trusted in his God.

Daniel 6: 15-16, 19-23, NLT

Being a different thinker saved Daniel from the lions. What he did exalted the name of the Lord. He made God known throughout the world as the God of the impossible:

Then King Darius sent this message to the people of every race and nation and language throughout the world… "I decree that everyone throughout my kingdom should tremble with fear before the God of Daniel.

"For he is the living God, and he will endure forever. His kingdom will never be destroyed, and his rule will never end. He rescues and saves his people; he performs miraculous signs and wonders in the heavens and on earth. He has rescued Daniel from the power of the lions."

Daniel 6: 25-27, NLT

Different thinking has a way of working wonders, because you set a platform from which God can operate. You provoke God to action. You learn to leave everything in the hands and care of God. You place yourself out there for impossibilities to turn into possibilities.

Fortunes are made out of misfortunes

A different thinker sees opportunities in the bleakest prospects. He can see possibilities in an abandoned piece of land that everyone else has dismissed as worthless. The next thing you know, he has bought it and built a five-star hotel or mega shopping complex on it.

To become a different thinker, start working on your thought patterns. Reprogram your mind: replace old thoughts of fear and doubt with thoughts of faith and hope. Persist in doing this with full commitment and undivided attention until the way of faith becomes a habit for you, an ingrained part of your character and lifestyle.

Many people have "trained" themselves to think negatively. They make it a habit to scrutinize everything, to look for something to be unhappy about in every situation. They can't rest until they have found something to moan about. They can't believe that things can be all good. They worry when they see the slightest sign of trouble brewing, and they worry even more when they don't see any trouble at all—because they fear that the trouble might manifest itself later. These people are perpetual worriers, even when there is nothing to worry about.

Do not be like them. Make it a habit to scrutinize every negative situation and come up with something good about it. Always look for the positive in the negative, even if it is like looking for a needle in a haystack—a feat that, though not at all easy, is actually not impossible either. Keep believing that fortunes can be made from unfortunate situations. Those unfortunate situations don't determine when the game is over for you, if you will just stay in the game until you win.

The man who stopped the sun and moon

As Moses' successor, Joshua's main task was to lead the Israelites across the Jordan River and possess the Promised Land. And he did just that. He believed that God could do the impossible: stop the Jordan River when it was in full flood, so that the people could cross over (*Joshua 3:1-17*); cause the walls of Jericho to fall down without any Israelite laying a finger on them (*Joshua 6:1-21*); and make the sun and moon stand still, so that the Israelites could finish the job of killing off their enemies (*Joshua 10:9-14*).

> As the men of Israel were pursuing and harassing the foe, Joshua prayed aloud, "Let the sun stand still over Gibeon, and let the moon stand in its place over the valley of Aijalon!"
>
> And the sun and the moon didn't move until the Israeli army had finished the destruction of its enemies... So the sun stopped in the heavens and stayed there for almost twenty-four hours! There had never been such a day before, and there has never been another since, when the Lord stopped the sun and moon—all because of the prayer of one man.
>
> *Joshua 10:12-14*

What is mind-blowing is that Joshua commanded the impossible to happen, and it did. He simply spoke it into existence. It was truly out of this world; the Bible tells us that there has never been anything like it before or since, when God stopped the sun and moon—all because one man dared to ask!

God had said to him right from the start, "I will be with you just as I was with Moses; I will not abandon you or fail to help you..." (*Joshua 1:5*). He simply took God at His word.

When God said, "Be strong and brave, for you will be a successful leader of my people; and they shall conquer all the land I promised to their ancestors" (*Joshua 1: 6*), he took God's word seriously, and it worked wonders for him.

Remember that Joshua was an army general. He had led the Israelite army to fight and conquer powerful nations on their way to the Promised Land. He was used to being in command. He understood the power, authority and control that came with his position as a general. He understood that it wasn't limited only to commanding people; it could be applied to every situation in life. He understood that he had the power and ability to command things to be the way he wanted. This was the reason he believed he could command the sun and the moon to stand still, and he was right.

Keep your eyes on the Master

When Peter saw his Master walking on the water, he was blown away. Though "reality" told him it was an impossible thing to do, he wanted to try it—because Jesus had done it! He had seen his Master doing the impossible and believed he could do the same—all the more because Jesus had encouraged him to step out of the boat and take that one step of faith into the water (*Matthew 14:29*).

Peter started well, but then fear and doubt crept in— when he took his eyes off his Master and fixed them on the wind. This made him forget the reason he thought it was possible to walk on the water. He started sinking because he was afraid. He was afraid because his focus was now on the wind buffeting the waves. He started to consider the impossibility and the awkwardness of what he was doing. He couldn't believe he was doing it. The wind scared the faith and courage out of him. That was where he messed up.

Peter went over the side of the boat and walked on the water toward Jesus. But when he saw the strong wind and the waves, he was terrified and began to sink. "Save me, Lord!" he shouted.

Jesus immediately reached out and grabbed him. "You have so little faith," Jesus said. "Why did you doubt me?"

Matthew 14:30-31, NLT

We can start well too, and find ourselves messing up along the way. Like Peter, we often allow the winds of adversity to scare the faith and courage out of us. What we need to learn is to keep our eyes on the Master and not give in to fears and doubts. Notice that Peter started to sink *after* he took his eyes off Jesus and began to look at the wind and waves. Jesus reached out at once and grabbed him. "Why did you doubt me?" He asked. Never doubt our Lord and God.

Thinking out of the box

Samaria was under siege by the Syrian army and no food supplies could be brought into the city. This resulted in a great famine, with women eating up their own children! And what was the king doing about this whole situation? He was blaming God! "The Lord has caused this mess," he stormed. "Why should I expect any help from him?" (*2 Kings 6:33*)

Contrast the king's attitude with Elisha's. Here was a prophet with absolute faith and trust in God. He could see provision and abundance in the midst of desperate lack. He told the people, "Tomorrow, about this time, there will be food again in Samaria." Where was the food going to come from, and how was it going to get to Samaria in such a short time? The prophet did not know. But he was certain that the impossible was about to give way to the possible.

Tomorrow? Many didn't believe it. It wasn't practical. It was ridiculous; too good to be true. One man even made fun of Elisha. "That couldn't happen even if the LORD opened the windows of heaven!" he mocked. Now, this man was an officer close to the king. He was regarded as a leader, but he was a blind leader. He had no vision. He was spiritually and mentally limited. He was thinking inside the box.

To him, it was simply and unquestionably impossible: how could something come out of nothing and from nowhere? How could they reap where they hadn't sown? This was Elisha's response to him: "You will see it happen with your own eyes, but you won't be able to eat any of it!" But there were those who believed the man of God and got to enjoy the food—because, true enough, it did arrive the next day, just as Elisha had said it would.

The way the food was provided was truly miraculous: four starving lepers were walking up to the Syrian camp, but God amplified the noise of their approach to seem like the sound of speeding chariots, galloping horses, and a vast army on the move. "They have hired the Hittites and Egyptians to attack us," the Syrians cried out. So, they panicked and fled, leaving behind a huge amount of food as well as gold, silver and many other treasures.

It took a different thinker to believe that the food could come so expeditiously; to understand that this was possible with God, who could provide through any means He chose that would bring glory to His name. A different thinker saved the whole of Samaria because he could see the solution where others only saw the problem. He could see provision in the midst of nothing. He could see the food— food that they didn't have to work for—coming their way.

As for the officer who had mocked Elisha, he never got to taste one bit of that food. He was killed in a stampede as the people scrambled for the food. He saw it, but he never got to eat it—just as the prophet had predicted. He died looking at others enjoying the food God had provided. He died seeing the fulfilment of Elisha's prophecy.

That officer had issues with people who thought out of the box; they didn't fit into his world. He didn't believe in miracles. He was one of those who thought miracles no longer happened; he couldn't comprehend the greatness of God. He died because of limited thinking. His lack of faith cost him his life. What a terrible death! What a sad ending!

Now, let us look at another man who had difficulty thinking out of the box—at first—but he didn't stay that way all his life. He did eventually change and become a different thinker. That man was Moses. When God called him to lead the Israelites out of slavery, his initial response was to reject the assignment.

"But I'm not the person for a job like that!" he protested (*Exodus 3:11*). Many miracles later—and this included the ten plagues God inflicted on Egypt (*Exodus chapters 7-12*) and the parting of the Red Sea (*Exodus 14: 21-31*)—it dawned on him that he needed to think differently. He needed to see things the way God saw them. The turning point for him came after God had delivered the Israelites out of Egypt and brought them into the desert.

They had run out of food by then and were on the verge of starving to death. The irony was that they had plenty of money to buy food because God had moved the Egyptians to be generous to them and give them all the silver and gold they asked for. But they couldn't buy anything in the wilderness. They were crying to Moses and demanding to be fed.

"Oh, that we were back in Egypt," they moaned... "For there we had plenty to eat. But now you have brought us into this wilderness to kill us with starvation."

Then the Lord said to Moses, "Look, I'm going to rain down food from heaven for them. Everyone can go out each day and gather as much food as he needs..."

Exodus 16:3-4

Food raining down from heaven? It had never happened before! It was a complete shock to them. But a different thinker would have understood that this was a small thing with God. God is always doing a new thing. He can put an army to flight and end a severe famine. He can rain down bread and meat from heaven to feed a whole nation.

Moses knew God's track record: how He had delivered the Israelites from a terrible bondage spanning more than 430 years. After all, he was the one spearheading the exodus out of Egypt! He had already witnessed all the mighty deeds God had done. What else could be so impossible for God to do, when He had already performed so many miracles for them? Indeed, God did for Israel exactly what He promised. Not a single word from His mouth went unfulfilled.

That evening vast numbers of quail flew in and covered the camp. And the next morning the area around the camp was wet with dew. When the dew evaporated, a flaky substance as fine as frost blanketed the ground.

The Israelites were puzzled when they saw it. "What is it?" they asked... They had no idea what it was.

And Moses told them, "It is the food the Lord has given you to eat.

Exodus 16:13-15, NLT

Many people struggle with unbelief, even after all they have seen God do for them. Like the Israelites, we have many wonderful testimonies of what our God has done for us, but we continue to doubt His power and ability. It is a common human failing: our current trials often cause us to forget the wonderful things God has done for us previously.

We have seen His miracles of healing, but we find it so difficult to believe He can provide for our needs. We have enjoyed His faithful provision, but we still wonder if He can heal our sicknesses. We have seen Him deliver us from grievous bondages, but a small problem can still destroy the mustard-seed faith we have.

We are like Thomas, who was with Jesus for three years and saw the greatest miracles of all time, but still battled with the demons of unbelief. Jesus had told the disciples before His death, "I, the Messiah, must suffer much and be killed; and three days later I will come back to life again!"

But Thomas didn't believe the other disciples when they told him they had seen the Lord after His resurrection. He was walking by sight and not by faith. He said, "I won't believe it unless I see the nail wounds in his hands—and put my fingers into them—and place my hand into his side."

Some days later, Jesus appeared to him and said, ""Put your finger into my hands. Put your hand into my side. Don't be faithless any longer. Believe!" It was only then that Thomas believed. Then Jesus said to him, "You believe because you have seen me. But blessed are those who haven't seen me and believe anyway" (*John 20:27, 29*).

The question is: why wasn't Thomas ready for this kind of news? Didn't he grasp the truth of what Jesus had been telling His disciples concerning His Resurrection—even before His death?

A forward-looking mindset

Only one thought occupies the mind of a different thinker every time he faces trials or challenges, and that is *success*. He holds this thought of success tenaciously in his mind. He gets excited about the possibilities he sees in every situation and refuses to entertain thoughts of failure. He has a way of seeing the success he wants to see, even if circumstances suggest otherwise. However, even if that success is not immediately forthcoming, he is not shaken.

Even if things go wrong somewhere along the way, he knows this does not define who he is. He knows he can start all over again. He knows he will have other opportunities to win. He understands that there are second chances in life. But, even if life doesn't give him that second chance, he will not give up; he will create opportunities for himself.

When your plan doesn't work out the way you expected, don't call it a failure; call it a learning experience. Take it as a blip, a bump in the road, a hurdle to overcome. Don't let it take you out of the game. It can turn out to be a valuable experience—just what you need to prepare you for that major assignment or breakthrough coming your way.

Learn from every experience—the good, the bad, and the ugly—and move on. Tap from yesterday's lessons to make today better, but don't dwell on the mistakes of the past or waste your time wallowing in regrets or self-pity. Let go of the past and move on, keeping your eyes on the end result you want to accomplish.

The apostle Paul never allowed himself to be held captive by the past. He was always looking to the future, and this inspired and energized him to move forward and to achieve the greater victories he always saw ahead of him.

He acknowledged that he had made mistakes in the past. But that did not deter him from pressing on and bringing all his energies to bear on one thing alone: *success*, which to him was winning the race of life and receiving his eternal reward from God. This was what he said to the Philippians:

> I don't mean to say I am perfect. I haven't learned all I should even yet, but I keep working toward that day when I will finally be all that Christ saved me for and wants me to be.
>
> No, dear brothers, I am still not all I should be, but I am bringing all my energies to bear on this one thing: Forgetting the past and looking forward to what lies ahead, I strain to reach the end of the race and receive the prize for which God is calling us up to heaven because of what Christ Jesus did for us.
>
> *Philippians 3:12-14*

A different thinker understands that yesterday is gone and he needs to make the most of today so that he can make his tomorrow better. He understands that his tomorrow is mainly determined by the kind of yesterday and today that he has gone through and learnt from. This motivates him to use the lessons of yesterday and today for the betterment of today. He knows that what he is seeing today cannot be compared to the future glory that will be revealed, for the greatest is still to come, and it *will* come tomorrow.

CHAPTER 2

Sees Something Out of Nothing

A DIFFERENT THINKER VISUALIZES THINGS INTO EXISTENCE. He is able to do this because he *believes that something can come out of nothing.* This leads him to *expect* to see things coming into existence that weren't there before. As he keeps believing in these expectations and visualizing them, he develops the confidence, courage and strength to work on the "nothing" which life has thrown at him and bring out of it the "something" that he wants. This doesn't come easily, though. He has to train his mind to envisage the things he wants. It takes faith to hold on to mental pictures of what you want until they manifest themselves in the physical.

It takes faith to visualize yourself as the father of a great nation when you don't have any children, and you and your wife are already past the age of child-bearing. It takes faith to see yourself having a baby while remaining a virgin. It takes faith to envision into existence large vats of the finest wine when there's only water around you. It takes faith to see yourself winning a fight with a giant, when you are a just a lad with nothing in your hand but five small stones and a sling. It takes faith to see opportunities where others see only opposition.

These are all true stories of people who made history because they had the faith to visualize the impossible and bring it into existence. In this chapter, we are going to discover how they did it—and learn to do likewise.

Would you have done what he did?

"Abraham!" God called... "Take with you your only son—yes, Isaac whom you love so much—and go to the land of Moriah and sacrifice him there as a burnt offering upon one of the mountains which I'll point out to you!"

The next morning Abraham got up early, chopped wood for a fire upon the altar, saddled his donkey, and took with him his son Isaac... When they arrived at the place where God had told Abraham to go, he built an altar and placed the wood in order, ready for the fire, and then tied Isaac and laid him on the altar over the wood. And Abraham took the knife and lifted it up to plunge it into his son, to slay him.

Genesis 22:1-3; 22:9

Abraham obeyed God and went ahead to sacrifice his only son because he believed that, even if Isaac died, God would make sure he still had a son in the end. He recalled that, long before Isaac was born, God had already promised him, "I am going to give you so many descendants that, like dust, they can't be counted" (*Genesis 13:16*). Abraham knew that God had to keep that promise—which was why he believed that, even if he sacrificed his son, God would raise Isaac up from the dead. He knew God wouldn't allow his only son to remain dead, since that would mean not having all those numerous descendants God had promised him.

Abraham saw the possibility of life coming out of death. He stood firmly on God's promise that he would become the father of a great nation (*Genesis 12:12*). What Abraham did —"you have not withheld even your beloved son from me" (*Genesis 22:12*)—touched the heart of God, and He provided a ram for him to sacrifice instead of his son (*Genesis 22:13*).

God was moved because Abraham was a different thinker. Not many would have done what Abraham did; most would have refused to sacrifice their children. Or, if they did initially agree to it, they would have backed out of it upon further reflection. They would have argued or bargained with God. They wouldn't have been able to see anything good coming out of such a situation—quite the opposite, in fact, since it would seem that obeying God would mean the end of everything for them.

Not so Abraham: he remembered the long years of barrenness and waiting, and how his wife Sarah had laughed when God told them He was going to give them a son. It had sounded ridiculous—too good to be true —because she was long past the age of childbearing. But God was faithful: Sarah had Isaac when she was ninety. Abraham himself was already a hundred years old by then. Yes, the God who could raise a dead womb to bear a living baby could surely raise a dead boy to life again!

An ordinary thinker would have berated God: "Why should I have had to wait so long for a son, only to lose him years later as a sacrifice? What then is the point of giving him to us in the first place? This doesn't make any sense at all. Where are the descendants to come from, that are going to be as numerous as the dust of the earth, if this only son is to be sacrificed? Where is the great nation that has been promised going to come from, when this boy is dead?"

But, in a situation like this, Abraham remembered the promises of God. This was what the Lord had said to him when Sarah laughed at the idea of bearing a child in her old age: "Is anything too hard for God?" (*Genesis 18:14*). Abraham understood that there was nothing too hard for

God to do. The Bible tells us that "'Abraham believed God, and God counted him as righteous because of his faith.' He was even called the friend of God" (*James 2:23, NLT*). Would you like God to call you His friend?

"Abraham My friend," (*Isaiah 41:8, NKJV*): that was what God called the man who trusted Him even when it made no sense to do so. Their friendship had begun long before Isaac was born, back in the days when Abraham was still living in the city of Haran, and God appeared to him and said:

> "Leave your own country behind you, and your own people, and go to the land I will guide you to. If you do, I will cause you to become the father of a great nation; I will bless you and make your name famous, and you will be a blessing to many others. I will bless those who bless you and curse those who curse you; and the entire world will be blessed because of you."
>
> *Genesis 12:1-4*

When God told Abraham to get out and go to a country that was totally unknown to him, he just went. No questions, no hesitation. He had to leave everything he knew behind him to start a new life and be established by God. What a wonderful thing to be established by God Almighty! The Bible tells us, "Believe in the Lord your God and you shall be established" (*2 Chronicles 20:20, AMPC*). Abraham took God at His word and was established by Him.

He didn't take God's promises for granted. He knew he needed to obey so that a great nation could come out of him. He needed to obey so that he could be blessed and be a blessing to all the families on the earth. He needed to fully believe and trust God so that he could receive all that God had promised him, including his inheritance from God.

Abraham trusted God, and when God told him to leave home and go far away to another land that he promised to give him, Abraham obeyed. Away he went, not even knowing where he was going... because he was confidently waiting for God to bring him to that strong heavenly city whose designer and builder is God.

Hebrews 11:8, 10

He was a stranger in strange places because he was looking for a city whose architect and builder is God. Ordinary thinkers would not have done what he did. But Abraham was looking for something out of the ordinary; something out of this world. And God said, because you are a different thinker, I will also outdo myself on your behalf:

"I, the Lord, have sworn by myself that because you have obeyed me and have not withheld even your beloved son from me, I will bless you with incredible blessings and multiply your descendants into countless thousands and millions, like the stars above you in the sky, and like the sands along the seashore. They will conquer their enemies, and your offspring will be a blessing to all the nations of the earth—all because you have obeyed me."

Genesis 22:16-18

It is always possible for something to come from nothing. The Israelites went into the Promised Land empty-handed. They had nothing, and God gave them everything. They took over cities they didn't develop; lived in houses they didn't build; drank from wells they didn't dig; reaped and ate what they didn't sow. Yes, good things *can* come from nothing if you have the faith to believe and the vision to see!

Behind the great Man is a great woman

Imagine that you are a teenage girl, just going about your day, when suddenly an angel appears and tells you, "You are going to have a baby!" Now the thing is, there's no way this could possibly happen, for the simple reason that you are *virgo intacta*—and intend to keep it that way until your marriage. Would you believe the angel?

Now, this really did happen to a girl called Mary. The angel Gabriel appeared to her and said, "Congratulations… God has decided to wonderfully bless you! Very soon now, you will become pregnant and have a baby boy."

Naturally enough, Mary's response was, ""But how can I have a baby? I am a virgin."

Now comes the incredible part: the angel replied, "The Holy Spirit shall come upon you, and the power of God shall overshadow you; so the baby born to you will be utterly holy—the Son of God" (*Luke 1:35*).

This was strange news indeed. Never had she heard of anyone having a baby while still a virgin. But Mary chose to believe the angel. It might sound impossible to others, but she saw the possibility of it happening. She said at once, ""I am the Lord's servant, and I am willing to do whatever he wants. May everything you said come true" (*Luke 1:38*).

Mary was a different thinker. She could see it happening exactly as the angel had said— "you will have a baby boy"— even though it seemed impossible in the natural order of things. This was why she sang a song of praise to God after receiving His message, when what was promised had yet to manifest itself in the physical: "Oh, how I praise the Lord… now generation after generation forever shall call me blest of God" (*Luke 1:46, 48*). And it happened exactly as the angel had said: Mary gave birth to Jesus, the Son of God (*Luke 2:6*).

Many years later, it was Mary who was the mastermind behind the first miracle that Jesus performed in public. It happened in this way:

> Jesus' mother was a guest at a wedding in the village of Cana in Galilee, and Jesus and his disciples were invited too. The wine supply ran out during the festivities, and Jesus' mother came to him with the problem.
>
> *John 2:1-3*

It would have been embarrassing for the wedding couple to run out of wine for their guests. Mary knew the solution was right in their midst: *Jesus*. But what was His response?

> "I can't help you now," he said. "It isn't yet my time for miracles."
>
> But his mother told the servants, "Do whatever he tells you to."
>
> *John 2:4-5*

As His mother, Mary knew and understood Jesus more than any other human being. She knew that He had the power to do anything. She had been there for Him every step of the way and was always a big supporter of His. She saw herself as a steward to whom God had entrusted His Son. God had trusted her to handle His Son rightly and ensure that Jesus fulfill His purpose for coming to earth. She knew how to get Him to do what He was meant to do.

She understood the time had come for Him to start His ministry. He needed to perform that first miracle for Him to be introduced to the world. Jesus said that His time for miracles had not yet come. But Mary wasn't convinced. She was sure that the hour had come for Him to do the works of His Father.

This was a different thinker indeed. She wasn't taking no for an answer. She knew there was a possibility for a yes. She persisted in what she believed in: that the wine shouldn't run out and spoil the day for the wedding couple —not when there was Someone in their midst who had the power to help them out.

She knew there had to be a solution to this embarrassing situation. She knew there was Someone in their midst who could make something out of nothing. She saw wine where there was no wine. She ignored the answer Jesus gave her and told the servants, "Do whatever he tells you to." She was determined to get what she wanted from her son. Mary received a negative answer from Jesus, but she turned it into a positive report. Because of this, Jesus told the servants to fill six big pots with water. That was it, and the rest is history; they had the best wine ever:

> When the master of ceremonies tasted the water that was now wine, not knowing where it had come from... he called the bridegroom over.
>
> "This is wonderful stuff!" he said. "You're different from most. Usually a host uses the best wine first, and afterwards, when everyone is full and doesn't care, then he brings out the less expensive brands. But you have kept the best for the last!"
>
> *John 2:9-10*

This was the first of many miracles that Jesus performed in the course of His ministry. It wouldn't have happened if not for Mary's belief that He could do it. The world needs people like her: exceptional thinkers who can see something, some hidden talent or potential, in those accounted as nothing by society; who can spur others on to do great things in life.

How to feed thousands from one lunchbox

Huge crowds followed Jesus wherever He went. Once, He was preaching to thousands of people out in the wilderness, and they got very hungry. But there was nothing to eat in that lonely place. The disciples were at a loss; it was impossible to provide food for so many people! Or so they thought.

Then Andrew, one of the disciples, reported, "There's a youngster here with five barley loaves and a couple of fish! But what good is that with all this mob?" (*John 6:8-9*)

What good are five small loaves and two tiny fish? That's how an ordinary thinker would view the situation. Andrew was among the twelve men chosen by Jesus to walk closely with Him, but that didn't seem to have opened his eyes to who Jesus really was and what He was capable of.

Andrew was still held captive by limited thinking and lack of faith. He was walking with God daily, but that had no effect on his thought life. He still retained the negative mindset he had before he became one of the chosen. He had no revelation of what his calling as an apostle signified. In fact, he had no revelation, even, of the kind of God he was following. He wasn't walking by faith but by sight.

Andrew was always with Christ, but he didn't have the mind of Christ in him. He didn't die to his old self when he started following the Lord; Andrew himself still lived. He wasn't like Paul, who could say, "I have been crucified with Christ: and I myself no longer live, but Christ lives in me" (*Galatians 2:20*). What Paul meant was that his old self had died, and he was now a new creation in Christ. As a new creation, he had put away all his old ways and embraced the new Way of Christ (*2 Corinthians 5:17*). This included his thinking: he now thought differently from his old self; he now thought like Christ. He was now a different thinker.

Many of us are like Andrew and the other disciples who battled with unbelief while they were with Jesus. We can understand why they struggled in their faith; they didn't know what we know today. We have the complete Bible. We have the Holy Spirit to help us. They only received the Holy Spirit at Pentecost. So, we should do better than them.

We have the Holy Spirit as our Teacher, Helper and Comforter. It is the Holy Spirit who reveals to us everything we need to know; who ignites our love and passion for God and what concerns Him; who gives us wisdom to serve God and to handle life in general. The Holy Spirit is able to do more than we can ever think or imagine, but most of us have a limited understanding of who He is, what He can do, and what He is here for. We underrate Him. We don't seek His help in everything but limit Him to just a few things. We limit Him to the confines of the church walls. Some even believe He is meant only for ministers of the gospel.

So, we put Him aside while we struggle with life. We fail to understand He is our Helper. When we struggle in prayer, He is the One who helps us: He prays for and in us according to the Father's will. He helps us pray relevant and effective prayers. The day you realize how crucial it is to seek after the Person of the Holy Spirit and involve Him fully in your life, that is the day everything will change radically for you.

> For we don't even know what we should pray for nor how to pray as we should, but the Holy Spirit prays for us with such feeling that it cannot be expressed in words. And the Father who knows all hearts knows, of course, what the Spirit is saying as he pleads for us in harmony with God's own will.
>
> *Romans 8:26-27*

Many of us underestimate the power of praying in the spirit. We don't pray often enough in the language the Holy Spirit has given us—by this, I mean in tongues. Some of us can pray for hours with our understanding (mind), but we can't take even five minutes of praying in the spirit. But why should we continue to pray only with our understanding, or let it dominate our prayers, when we can gain so much more by also praying in the spirit? The Word of God encourages us to pray both with the spirit and also with the mind (understanding); but one is more vital than the other:

> Then what am I to do? I will pray with my spirit [by the Holy Spirit that is within me], but I will also pray [intelligently] with my mind and understanding...
>
> *1 Corinthians 14:15, AMPC*

I would like you to study this verse carefully; I believe the order in which the sentences were arranged was done intentionally. In particular, study what the word "also" suggests as to the primary way we should be praying. "Also" is defined in the dictionary as "in addition"; it means "too", "moreover", "as well"—something that is secondary. Take time to think about this; the insights you draw from it will determine the state and success of your spiritual life.

Now, you may be wondering: if praying in the spirit is so essential, why are we not doing more of it? Why are we praying so much more with our understanding? The short answer is this: often, it is because of too much asking. Most of our prayers are self-centred. Everything is about us. It is about receiving and receiving, nothing more. When we pray, it is simply because we have a request to bring to God. We pray for things we know about. But praying in tongues is praying for unknown things; it is speaking mysteries.

> For one who speaks in an unknown tongue does not speak to people but to God; for no one understands him or catches his meaning, but by the Spirit he speaks mysteries [secret truths, hidden things].
>
> *1 Corinthians 14:2, AMP*

When you pray in tongues, you are not speaking to men but to God. For us to see the will of God done on earth as it is in heaven, we need to speak the language of the Holy Spirit. For the kingdom of God to come into our hearts and into this world, we need to pray more in the spirit. There is no way you can excel in ministry if you don't pray in the spirit.

When you speak the language of the Holy Spirit, you are speaking mysteries. You are communicating with God. You are speaking the language heaven understands best. You are invoking the Creator of all creation. You are going beyond the natural realm and gaining access to the supernatural. You are bringing the supernatural into the natural. You are bringing the physical manifestation of the spiritual things. You are connecting with heaven and getting heavenly backup. You are preparing a platform for God to act and do what He knows best.

Praying in tongues builds up our faith (*Jude 1:20*). It is a gift from the Holy Spirit, but many Christians underutilize it—or don't even use it at all. And this is the reason we live defeated lives. This is the reason we face the future with so much fear and doubt. This is the reason many are struggling with limitations in their ministries and lives in general. This is the reason the world is the way it is. We need to change all this. We need to fully utilize this gift of tongues, the way the Holy Spirit meant it to be used. Our lives will turn out for the better, the day we decide to do this.

Let us now turn our attention back to the hungry hordes out there in the wilderness:

> "Tell everyone to sit down," Jesus ordered. And all of them—the approximate count of the men only was five thousand—sat down on the grassy slopes.
>
> Then Jesus took the loaves and gave thanks to God and passed them out to the people. Afterwards he did the same with the fish. And everyone ate until full!
>
> "Now gather the scraps," Jesus told his disciples, "so that nothing is wasted." And twelve baskets were filled with the leftovers!
>
> *John 6:10-13*

Amazing! Five thousand men. But that's not the whole story. There were women there too—the wives of those men, the widows and the other single women—although no headcount was taken of them. And there were also the children. So, the total number of people was many thousands more. And after everyone had eaten their fill, they still had twelve baskets of food left over. *All this from five loaves and two fish.* And all because Jesus was a different thinker. He wasn't limited by the limitations of this world; He could see something—many things—coming out of virtually nothing.

A grasshopper mentality

God told Moses, "Send spies into the land of Canaan—the land I am giving to Israel" (*Numbers 13:2*). So, Moses sent out twelve spies, among whom were Joshua and Caleb. These two men stood out. They had independent minds. They maintained their faith even when the other ten spies returned from Canaan with a negative report. They weren't influenced by the limited thinking of the majority.

Ten spies came back from Canaan with a report that struck fear into the hearts of the Israelites:

> "The land is full of warriors, the people are powerfully built, and we saw some of the Anakim there, descendants of the ancient race of giants. We felt like grasshoppers before them, they were so tall!"
>
> *Numbers 13:32-33*

Compare this with the report given by the other two spies, Joshua and Caleb:

> "It is a wonderful country ahead, and the Lord loves us. He will bring us safely into the land and give it to us. It is very fertile, a land 'flowing with milk and honey'! Oh, do not rebel against the Lord, and do not fear the people of the land. For they are but bread for us to eat! The Lord is with us and he has removed his protection from them! Don't be afraid of them!"
>
> *Numbers 14:7-9*

Incredible! How could twelve men have seen the exact same things but seen them so differently? Ten men saw only the worst of the situation, whilst the other two saw the best of it. God had already said He was going to give Canaan to the Israelites, but those ten spies still clung on to their fears and doubts. They didn't trust the Promise Giver.

These are people who will never achieve greatness. They have a habit of exaggerating the negative aspects of every situation. They magnify small issues to seem like the biggest challenges. An ant can look like an elephant to them. A stone becomes a hill; and a hill, a mountain. This is a serious flaw because you mainly achieve according to the measure of your faith and your mental picture of what the outcome will be.

They believed that nothing good would come from any attempt to conquer Canaan. Yes, they acknowledged that it was "indeed a magnificent country—a land 'flowing with milk and honey'" (*Numbers 13:27*). They even brought back some of the fruit as proof of how fertile the land was; one example was the "single cluster of grapes so large that it took two of them to carry it on a pole between them" (*Numbers 13:23*).

In effect, they were saying, "It's a great country, but greater still is the danger of trying to take it. There's something here we should consider more than the milk and honey; more than the biggest, juiciest fruit we have ever seen."

> "But the people living there are powerful, and their cities are fortified and very large; and what's more, we saw Anakim giants there!"
>
> *Numbers 13:28*

They were not even going to try to fight those giants. "Why bother? We're going to lose, anyway," they said. "We don't see ourselves coming out as victors but as victims. We are so much smaller than the giants living there, *we even feel like grasshoppers compared to them*!" This was their mindset.

The truth of the matter was that they had exaggerated the size of those giants: the Anakim were in reality nowhere as tall as the spies had made them out to be—at least not to the extent that a normal-size man could look like a grasshopper when standing beside them. But those men had already programmed their minds to expect defeat.

Their negative report created an uproar throughout the Israelite camp. All the people cried and grumbled and turned against their leaders, Moses and Aaron. This is always the case with people who have a negative attitude or a habit of magnifying problems.

Then all the people began weeping aloud, and they carried on all night. Their voices rose in a great chorus of complaint against Moses and Aaron.

"We wish we had died in Egypt," they wailed, "or even here in the wilderness, rather than be taken into this country ahead of us. Jehovah will kill us there, and our wives and little ones will become slaves."

Numbers 14:1-3

Once the Israelites started on this tack, there was no stopping them: they brought up old issues and reopened old wounds. They repeated what they had said when they faced the Red Sea (*Exodus 14:11-12*) and when they needed food (*Exodus 16:3*) and water (*Exodus 17:3*) in the wilderness: "It is better to have died in Egypt." Surprisingly, this time they said they preferred the wilderness; those other times, they wanted to get out of it. Confusion indeed.

Life hadn't been easy for them, out in the wilderness; but now that they were facing a different challenge, they said that staying in the wilderness was way better than fighting giants. Such is the contrariness of human nature; we don't want this thing because of that other thing, and then we realize we actually want it because of something else. The truth is, most of the time we don't know what we want, especially when we are facing challenges.

Then, matters started to get really out of hand. Rebellion swept through the camp as the people cried to one another, "Let's get out of here and return to Egypt... Let's elect a leader to take us back to Egypt!" At this, Moses and Aaron fell on their faces before the whole assembly. Joshua and Caleb, the only two who had brought back a positive report, tore their clothes as a sign of their grief (*Numbers 14:3-6*).

They couldn't believe that the Israelites actually wanted to go back to the kind of bondage they and their forefathers had been in for over four hundred and thirty years.

Just one negative report was all it took for the Israelites to forget everything God had done for them: how He had delivered them from slavery in Egypt, parted the Red Sea to save them from Pharaoh and his army, and protected them from their enemies in the wilderness. That report destroyed whatever little faith they had in God. They forgot His past faithfulness and all the miracles He had done for them.

But the mood was about to turn even uglier as the crowd started to talk about stoning Joshua and Caleb. What had triggered this was the two men's attempt to reassure the Israelites that they were well able to conquer Canaan because the Lord was with them. They warned the people not to rebel against God but to take possession of the land, as He had instructed them. This was what added salt to the wound; this was what drove the crowd to such a frenzy that they were on the verge of stoning the two men.

At that critical moment, God came down in all His glory. He *had* to intervene; the situation had reached a flashpoint:

> Then the glory of the Lord appeared, and the Lord said to Moses, "How long will these people despise me? Will they never believe me, even after all the miracles I have done among them?"
>
> *Numbers 14:10-11*

A lesson to be learnt here: we are not doing ourselves any good if we allow negative thinking to dominate our lives. Like those Israelites, we won't be able to reach the destiny God meant for us if we allow our minds to be paralyzed by negativity, doubt and fear.

A negative mentality has a way of making people victims of their circumstances. When you set limitations on your abilities, you are in effect incarcerating yourself in a prison of your own making. When you see yourself as a grasshopper and your challenges as giants, too formidable for you to overcome, you are depriving yourself of all you could have enjoyed—just like the generation of Israelites who were left to wander in the wilderness. Because of their negative attitude, they deprived themselves of the Promised Land that God had meant for their enjoyment. They lost it all:

> Then the Lord said... "Not a single one of you twenty years old and older, who has complained against me, shall enter the Promised Land. Only Caleb and Joshua are permitted to enter it.
>
> "You said your children would become slaves of the people of the land. Well, instead I will bring them safely into the land and they shall inherit what you have despised. But as for you, your dead bodies shall fall in this wilderness. You must wander in the desert like nomads for forty years. In this way you will pay for your faithlessness, until the last of you lies dead in the desert."
>
> *Numbers 14:26, 29-33*

Their real problem had nothing to do with the giants. Their real problem lay in their grasshopper mentality: "we felt like grasshoppers before those giants, they were so tall!" Many people today have a grasshopper mentality too. They blow up a small difficulty until it assumes gigantic proportions. They see hill-sized challenges as mountains and run away from them without even trying to climb them, because they are fully convinced that those mountains are too high for them to conquer.

The truth is that Joshua and Caleb were also exposed to the same intimidating situation as the other ten spies. They too saw those giants and warriors and their fortified cities, but they chose to see them differently because they had a different spirit (*Numbers 14:24*). They believed that God was able to deliver those giants into their hands and give them the land He had promised them.

> Caleb reassured the people as they stood before Moses. "Let us go up at once and possess it," he said, "for we are well able to conquer it!"
>
> "Not against people as strong as they are!" the other spies said. "They would crush us!"
>
> *Numbers 13:30-31*

> Then the ten spies who had incited the rebellion against Jehovah by striking fear into the hearts of the people were struck dead before the Lord. Of all the spies, only Joshua and Caleb remained alive.
>
> *Numbers 14:36-38*

Joshua and Caleb gained everything because they could see something coming out of nothing: they saw themselves living in houses they had not built, owning land they had not worked for, drinking from wells they had not dug, and eating from vineyards and olive groves they had not planted (*Deuteronomy 6:10-11; Joshua 24:10-11*). This vision fired them up so much that it drove out all fear of the giants. It made them eager to go up at once and possess the land. And all that they had envisioned—land, cities, houses, wells, vineyards, olive groves and much more—eventually became theirs to enjoy, when a new generation of Israelites went in and possessed the Promised Land forty years later.

The Israelites wandered about in the wilderness for the next forty years until that whole generation which had refused to enter Canaan had died out, and only Joshua and Caleb remained. By then, Moses had died too and Joshua had become the new leader of Israel—a very successful and prosperous leader indeed, for God was with him. Under Joshua's leadership, the Israelites conquered Canaan. Then, Caleb came to Joshua and reminded him of what God had promised forty years back—that the section of Canaan which Caleb had explored as a spy would be given to him:

> "Now, as you see, from that time until now the Lord has kept me alive and well for all these forty-five years …and today I am eighty-five years old. I am as strong now as I was when Moses sent us on that journey, and I can still travel and fight as well as I could then! So I'm asking that you give me the hill country that the Lord promised me... as spies we found the Anakim living there in great, walled cities, but if the Lord is with me, I shall drive them out of the land."
>
> So Joshua blessed him and gave him Hebron as a permanent inheritance because he had followed the Lord God of Israel.
>
> *Joshua 14:6-14*

God kept Caleb alive and strong for forty-five years, just to make sure he got what He had promised him—which goes to show that what we do for God is never in vain. In due season, we will reap our reward if we keep going and don't back down in the face of challenges. People may forget your labor but God never does. He is Jehovah Roi, the God who sees and knows everything about you (*Genesis 16:13*).

Giant or grasshopper mentality?

We all know the story of David and Goliath: how, as a young boy, David defeated Goliath, a seasoned warrior who was close to ten feet tall. And he did it with nothing more than a sling and a stone. This giant had been terrorizing the Israeli army and no one dared to fight him. But David didn't see Goliath the way the other Israelites saw him.

Those other Israelites saw Goliath as an invincible foe. And they saw themselves as grasshoppers, in much the same way as the ten spies had seen themselves many years earlier. But David saw himself as a *giant*, not a grasshopper. He saw himself killing Goliath and cutting off his head. He saw the whole scene taking place in the supernatural before anything at all had happened in the physical.

David saw himself differently from the other Israelites because he was a different thinker. Like Joshua and Caleb, he had a different spirit. He saw himself as a winner, victor and conqueror. He understood his true identity. He didn't hesitate to speak his mind about what he believed of himself. He wouldn't back down or apologize to anyone for how he saw himself—even though this made his faith and courage seem like pride to his eldest brother Eliab:

> Eliab's anger was aroused against David, and he said, "Why did you come down here? And with whom have you left those few sheep in the wilderness? I know your pride and the insolence of your heart, for you have come down to see the battle."
>
> And David said, "What have I done now? Is there not a cause?" Then he turned from him…
>
> *1 Samuel 17:28-30, NKJV*

David was too determined to be discouraged, too confident to be put down by his brother's criticism. This determination and confidence arose out of his conscious decision to see things differently. Perhaps, when David first caught sight of Goliath, the man did seem gigantic to him. But David decided to take another look. Then a closer look. Followed by an even closer look. He rubbed his eyes and stared hard at the giant. This time, Goliath didn't seem so big anymore.

Under David's intense scrutiny, the giant appeared to be shrinking... and shrinking... until what had seemed like a formidable foe at first sight now looked like any ordinary, average-size man in his eyes. This changed everything for David. Instead of looking up at the man as a colossus to be dreaded, he now looked down on him with disdain. He now saw Goliath as a grasshopper that he could destroy easily.

We can also put it this way: when David saw Goliath for the first time, he might have felt like a tiny grasshopper beside the giant. But everything changed when he decided to think and see things differently. Perhaps he took a close look at himself... then an even closer look, until at last he changed the way he saw himself. Out went the grasshopper mentality; it got deleted straightaway, and he now saw himself as a giant and a champion.

Of course, this transformed image of himself radically transformed the way he saw the giant too. In David's eyes, they swapped positions: the giant became a grasshopper, and the boy who used to be a grasshopper became a giant. The truth is that, when you have a grasshopper mentality, you can't defeat a giant. Only those with a giant mentality can defeat giants. There is no place for grasshoppers when it comes to a straight fight with giants.

Up till the moment when David killed Goliath, nobody in Israel or among the Philistines would ever have believed that the giant could lose a fight. Everyone, including Goliath himself, thought he was invincible—everyone except David. He was the only one who saw Goliath for what he really was: a swaggering bully on the outside, but a cowardly grasshopper within. When David first set eyes on him, the giant had already been taunting and terrorizing King Saul and the Israeli army for forty days:

> He stood and shouted across to the Israelis, "Do you need a whole army to settle this? I will represent the Philistines, and you choose someone to represent you, and we will settle this in single combat... I defy the armies of Israel! Send me a man who will fight with me!"
>
> When Saul and the Israeli army heard this, they were dismayed and frightened.
>
> *1 Samuel 17: 8, 10-11*

Goliath strutted before the armies of Israel, casting insults at them—and, by extension, at the God of Israel too. But no one dared to stand up to him; in fact, the whole army ran away in fright. David couldn't have just turned a blind eye to all this. He asked the people around him, "Who is this heathen Philistine, anyway, that he is allowed to defy the armies of the living God?" (*1 Samuel 17:26*)

That was when his brother Eliab got angry with him. He heard David talking like that and mistook the young boy's faith for arrogance. David, however, had a ready reply: "Is there not a cause?" There *was* a cause: he couldn't have just kept silent when God was being mocked. He had to step up to the plate and show Goliath and the Philistines that there was a God in Israel, and He was not to be trifled with!

When it was finally realized what David meant, someone told King Saul, and the king sent for him.

"Don't worry about a thing," David told him. "I'll take care of this Philistine!"

"Don't be ridiculous!" Saul replied. "How can a kid like you fight with a man like him? You are only a boy, and he has been in the army since he was a boy!"

But David persisted. "When I am taking care of my father's sheep," he said, "and a lion or a bear comes and grabs a lamb from the flock, I go after it with a club and take the lamb from its mouth.

"If it turns on me, I catch it by the jaw and club it to death. I have done this to both lions and bears, and I'll do it to this heathen Philistine too, for he has defied the armies of the living God!"

1 Samuel 17:31-37

Seeing victory everywhere

David had only one thought in his mind when he looked at the giant: *victory, victory, victory.* He saw, through eyes of faith, the word *victory* written everywhere. He saw his name being changed to *victory;* he saw *victory* before, behind and all over him. He saw *victory* every place he looked.

Remember the Madagascar film? Alex the lion had a habit of seeing the animals around him turning into steaks every time he got hungry. Hunger pangs drove him to see meat everywhere. Every time he looked at an animal, he saw it as a potential meal. This is what I mean when I say a person with a victor mentality sees victory everywhere. This was what happened to David too. He was hungry for victory, he had a victory mentality, and he saw victory everywhere.

This is evident from what he said to Goliath, just before he hurled the stone that killed the giant:

> "You come to me with a sword and a spear, but I come to you in the name of the Lord of the armies of heaven and of Israel—the very God whom you have defied. Today the Lord will conquer you, and I will kill you and cut off your head."
>
> *1 Samuel 17:45-46*

David knew that the One who was in him was greater than the one he was facing. He knew that the battle was not his but the Lord's. This was the reason he could defeat Goliath and his army. When the Philistines saw that their champion was dead, they ran away. They fled from a youngster, a rookie with no military training or experience whatsoever.

David went on to become the greatest king Israel ever had. He won every battle he fought because he trusted God wholeheartedly. He had a different spirit. He could see something coming out of nothing. He could see victory coming out of a situation in which others saw only defeat.

It is my desire that the stories I have shared in this book —of David and other different thinkers—will encourage you to become a different thinker too. Different thinking comes from being yourself. If we will all just be ourselves, we will automatically be different from one other—because we are all made to be different.

There is nothing wrong in having a different viewpoint or in following your own path in life; it is in fact the right and natural thing to do. Much can be gained if we all embrace our own uniqueness. Think how much more interesting the world would be! How many more problem solvers we would have! How many more giant killers!

In the footsteps of their master: a giant mentality

> There was also Benaiah… a heroic soldier from Kabzeel. Benaiah killed two giants… Another time he went down into a pit and, despite the slippery snow on the ground, took on a lion that was caught there and killed it.
>
> *2 Samuel 23:20*

Like gives birth to like. Giant killers give birth to other giant killers. So it was with David: he led by example and inspired the army officers serving under him to become men of faith and valor too. One of them was a warrior named Benaiah, who killed two giants and a lion. Obviously, this man didn't subscribe to the common belief that humans were not meant to take on giants and lions singlehandedly.

To put it another way, Benaiah saw himself differently; he saw himself as stronger than any giant or lion. Like his master David, he had only one thing in mind: *victory*. No ordinary man could have done what he did; they were the actions of a different thinker. His master's faith had rubbed off on him, and he was as brave and as bold as a lion.

He didn't rush foolhardily into danger either: as with David, there was a righteous cause each time he fought, and he was fully confident of God's backing. *Proverbs 28:1* tells us that "the godly are bold as lions". Benaiah's actions revealed his understanding of who God is and who he was in God. They showed the level of trust this man had in God.

Benaiah was just one of David's mighty warriors. Another was Josheb-Basshebeth, who once killed eight hundred men in one battle. I encourage you to read *2 Samuel 23* to find out more about the kind of men King David surrounded himself with—godly men who did great exploits because they had a victory mentality, just like their master David.

In the footsteps of our Master: the mind of Christ

To be a different thinker, you need to have the mind of Christ, which is the mind of God. When you have the mind of Christ, your thoughts and perceptions will be aligned with His and be different from those of the world.

What do we need to do to have the mind of Christ? Above all else, we need to have His Word in our lives. We need to be governed by His Word. This comes about when we diligently read, study and meditate on His Word, which is the Bible.

When we fill ourselves with His Word, we are filling ourselves with His thoughts and we begin to think like Him. We begin to receive divine revelations from His Word. We begin to do things His way. We are being led by the Spirit; and when we are walking in the Spirit, we are in the truth, for the Spirit is truth.

Conversely, whoever is not led by the Spirit is not in the truth. Whatever is done in the flesh is false; it is not done in faith. And, without faith, it is impossible to please God. The mind of the flesh, with its carnal thoughts and purposes, is hostile to God (*Romans 8:7*). To be carnally minded is death because the things of the flesh are temporal. But the things of the spirit are eternal.

To be spiritually minded is life and peace. This is because, when we are led by the Word of God and by the Spirit, we are made wiser than our enemies—and wiser even than our teachers and elders (*Psalm 119:98-100*). Wonderful truth indeed! But it doesn't easily. We have our part to play. We can only have the mind of Christ when God's Word becomes sovereign in our lives.

CHAPTER 3

Sees Solutions in Challenges

A DIFFERENT THINKER SEES SOLUTIONS IN CHALLENGES. Others may see only the problem, but he sees the solution looming large before his eyes and dwarfing the problem. Take the case of a faith-filled minister of the gospel: what does he do when a terminally ill man comes to him for help? The sick man sees this illness as a calamity looming as large as Mount Everest before him. He sees death staring him in the face. He sees death, not life, because he is an ordinary thinker. He has believed the report that this is a deadly disease. Therefore, he can't see anything else except the negativity surrounding this illness.

But the faith-filled minister is a different thinker. He praises the Lord because he sees the sick man being healed and enjoying good health. The healing he sees in his spirit dominates the sickness he sees in the physical realm. He sees life, not death. He magnifies the healing and minimizes the illness. He sees the problem—the sickness—and perceives that the solution—the miracle of healing—is an opportunity for God to reveal His power and glory.

This is what I mean when I say that a different thinker is able to see a solution greater than the crisis he faces. This ability enables him to face problems head on and not run away from them. It enables him to maintain his peace and joy, to praise God in the midst of trials, and to keep his composure because he is not overwhelmed by the situation.

Adverse circumstances may turn out to be a blessing in disguise. Many founders of business empires were once jobless. They couldn't find employment, so they became their own employer. Had they been able to find regular, well-paid work, they would probably not have taken the more difficult and riskier path of entrepreneurship.

Similarly, many bestselling authors started writing books only because they found themselves stuck at home without a job. They needed money; so, necessity being the mother of invention, they turned to inventing stories. Need, along with poverty, has also given birth to million-dollar inventions and discoveries—and sometimes because those inventors, being unemployed, had time on their hands to come up with new ideas.

By saying that a different thinker can see solutions in the midst of problems, I mean that he can see a gain where others see a loss. His family cries when he loses his job, but he rejoices because he now has time to start the business he has always dreamt of. He now has the opportunity to go where he has always wanted to go. He can now do what he has always wanted to do.

When a different thinker sees his house being burnt to the ground, he doesn't cry like those without hope. He understands that, though the tree is cut, the stump will grow again. He is already planning ahead and seeing himself as the owner of the newest, grandest home in town.

He knows that broken relationships can be mended and, better still, can be made stronger than before. We all know of couples or families that have separated and then got back together again. Their time apart had made them value each other more and given them a stronger determination to make the relationship work once they were reunited.

A different thinker knows that problems and solutions have a way of going hand in hand. We wouldn't have been able to enjoy the solution if we hadn't had the problem that needed solving in the first place. The same goes with success and failure: would success have any meaning at all if we hadn't first failed—and then persisted until we overcame all odds to achieve our goal?

A different thinker knows that challenges are not always as bad as they seem. He sees every challenge as a battleground where he can emerge with the spoils of war— the desired reward or solution which dominates his vision so compellingly that the challenge becomes by comparison a minor setback he can easily conquer.

Sleeping with lions

The truth is that sometimes God allows challenges to come into your life. And, no matter how you cry and plead with Him, He will not spare you; you will still have to go through those tough times. I am talking about challenges that have come about, not through any wrongdoing or foolhardiness on your part, but through no fault of your own—or perhaps because your enemies are doing all they can to destroy you. This was what happened to Daniel, the great man of God whom we first met in Chapter 1 of this book.

Remember the story of Daniel and how he was thrown into a den of lions? His enemies were looking for an excuse to get him into trouble with the king, but "they couldn't find anything to criticize! He was faithful and honest and made no mistakes" (*Daniel 6:4*). So, they resorted to trickery and got the king to throw Daniel to the lions. And God allowed it to happen. He could have stopped Daniel from going through the whole ordeal of facing those lions. But He didn't.

Daniel knew the challenge was not as bad as it seemed. He saw it as a battlefield from which he would emerge victorious, whatever the outcome—because he knew that, whether he lived or died, God's name would be glorified. And that was exactly what happened: God sent His angel to shut the lions' mouths, and Daniel slept with the lions and came out the next morning without so much as a scratch on him. What an amazing display of God's power!

Afterward King Darius wrote this message addressed to everyone in his empire:

"Greetings! I decree that everyone shall tremble and fear before the God of Daniel in every part of my kingdom. For his God is the living, unchanging God whose kingdom shall never be destroyed and whose power shall never end. He delivers his people, preserving them from harm; he does great miracles in heaven and earth; it is he who delivered Daniel from the power of the lions."

Daniel 6:25-27

Through this incident, the king saw for himself the power of Daniel's God. He saw the hand of God upon Daniel. Because of this, he held Daniel in high regard and promoted him to a top-ranking position. If Daniel hadn't gone through the challenge of facing those lions, he wouldn't have got that kind of promotion. Through it all, he never lost his faith in God; he never once asked God why He was throwing him to the lions. He knew that den of lions was his battlefield, from which he would emerge with the spoils of victory. And he did; he got his promotion and, better still, the name of God was glorified throughout the empire of King Darius.

Most of the time, we view challenges as unwelcome intrusions into the smooth tenor of our lives. We believe we would be better off without them. But the truth is that God has the right to do as He wills—and His will for us may sometimes include the very challenges we dread most. In fact, challenges are an inescapable part of everyone's life.

What we need when we are facing challenges is help from God, and it is up to Him how He chooses to help us. He may decide to take the situation away from us, or take us away from it, or take us *through* it. When we entrust ourselves to Him, believing that He knows best what to do, we will be able to face those challenges with peace and joy. We can be sure that His goodness and mercy will follow us all the days of our lives (*Psalm 23:6*), regardless of what we are going through.

Feasting in the presence of your foes

Like Daniel, David had many enemies who sought to kill him. For years before he became king, he was on the run and in mortal danger from King Saul and his men. Yet, David could declare confidently:

> The Lord is my light and my salvation; he protects me from danger—whom shall I fear? When evil men come to destroy me, they will stumble and fall!
>
> *Psalm 27:1-2*

David testified to the Lord preparing a table for him in the presence of his enemies (*Psalm 23:5*). This is also what God wants to do for us—to save and bless us while our enemies are watching. Imagine sitting down to a sumptuous feast prepared by God Himself! Imagine your enemies watching the show and fuming away but unable to do anything to you!

They can't interfere with what is going on at the table because God is in control. They can't do a thing except watch in fury and frustration. This is one reason God allows challenges to come into your life—to reveal His power and glory, and to demonstrate His ability to save and bless you.

> And now my head shall be lifted up above my enemies all around me...
>
> *Psalm 27:6, NKJV*

It is only when you are surrounded by enemies that your head can be lifted *above* them. When you are in the midst of opposition, you get to be the centre of attention, and what the Lord does for you becomes more noticeable. Your blessing becomes more evident when you are the only one whose head is lifted up or the only one feasting at the table.

Seeing the solution beyond the situation

God may provide a table of good things for you in full view of your foes, and sometimes you do get rewards while still in the thick of battle. These are solutions that come to you in the midst of challenges. But there are other solutions that you can only get *after* you have overcome those challenges. More often than not, the biggest rewards come only after a long, hard-won battle.

Take the case of an athlete competing in a race: he can't just stay home and expect to win the trophy. He needs to play his part by training hard and running his best race. It takes perseverance and hard work to be the first to cross the finishing line. This is true of everything in life: things of value have to be won by overcoming challenges of all kinds first. But most people just want the good things to fall into their laps without any sacrifice or striving on their part.

A different thinker knows that, to get what he wants, he has to put in the effort and persist to the end. As he runs his race, the long track ahead of him may loom larger than the trophy in the distance. But he sees beyond the immediate challenges of the race to the reward that will ultimately be his. In other words, he sees beyond the situation to the solution, and this spurs him on to win the race. This was also the mindset of the apostle Paul; he saw beyond his present suffering to the heavenly reward that he knew was awaiting him:

> I am bringing all my energies to bear on this one thing: Forgetting the past and looking forward to what lies ahead, I strain to reach the end of the race and receive the prize for which God is calling us up to heaven because of what Christ Jesus did for us.
>
> *Philippians 3:13-14*

"None of these things move me"

Everything Paul said and did showed that he was a different thinker. There was a time when he had a heart-to-heart talk with the elders of the Ephesian church—a talk that revealed and encapsulated his whole mission and mindset:

> And see, now I go bound in the spirit to Jerusalem, not knowing the things that will happen to me there, except that the Holy Spirit testifies in every city, saying that chains and tribulations await me.
>
> *But none of these things move me*; nor do I count my life dear to myself, so that I may finish my race with joy, and the ministry which I received from the Lord Jesus, to testify to the gospel of the grace of God.
>
> *Acts 20:22-24, NKJV*

Perils, persecution, prison and possibly death—*none of those things moved Paul!* He set his face resolutely to go to Jerusalem, much like his Master Jesus had done before him (see *Luke 9:51; Isaiah 50:7*). Like his Master, he did not count his life dear to himself.

On his way to Jerusalem, Paul passed through Caesarea, where he met a prophet named Agabus. This man took Paul's belt, bound his own feet and hands with it, and said, "The Holy Spirit declares, 'So shall the owner of this belt be bound by the Jews in Jerusalem and turned over to the Romans'" (*Acts 21:11*). Although Paul knew that the prophet was telling the truth, he still insisted on going to Jerusalem.

Everyone who heard the prophecy was troubled and begged him to change his mind. But Paul was undeterred; he declared, "I am ready not only to be bound, but also to die in Jerusalem for the name of the Lord Jesus" (*Acts 21:13, NIV*). These are clearly the words of a different thinker. They reveal the degree and kind of understanding Paul had about God and about his identity and purpose in life. This was a man who had gone beyond ordinary thinking and understanding. He lived for a cause and was ready to die for it.

One sign that shows you are a different thinker is when people around you do not readily accept the way you think or live your life. You don't fit into their world and may even find yourself in conflict with them. You may face conflicts in the workplace or in church, or with social institutions or the system or environment you are in. This is because, for the most part, the world is run by and for ordinary thinkers. They are satisfied with what is already in place and don't see any need for change or improvement. The standard has been set by ordinary thinkers, with mediocrity firmly established as the norm, and this is what limits progress.

But when a different thinker comes on the scene, he wonders why the goods he buys are of such inferior quality, why work is so shoddily done, and why poor service is the norm. He sees the need to raise the bar where others accept the status quo. He sees the need to confront and deal with issues whilst most people would rather let sleeping dogs lie. This is why he may find himself in conflict with them.

This was what happened with Paul too. People around him saw the prophecy as a warning to him not to go to Jerusalem because of all that he would suffer there. But Paul viewed the prophecy differently. He saw the bigger picture. Yes, he would suffer and most likely die too. But the gospel would be preached and God's name would be glorified, and that was all that mattered! You can say Paul really upped the ante when it came to serving God. It is rare to find people like him. If only there were more of them—more people who are willing to sacrifice their own self-interest for the larger good—what a better place the world would be!

Most of us want to be popular. We want people to like us, even to love us. If they don't, our whole world crumbles. But there is no guarantee that you will be accepted, much less loved by others, if you are a different thinker. On the contrary, many may not understand or approve of you. It is not as though the good you do would be appreciated by people. Some may even hate you for it—as they hated Paul.

There was a time when a crowd stoned Paul and dragged him out of the city, thinking he was dead (*Acts 14:19*). On another occasion, forty Jews vowed neither to eat nor drink until they had killed Paul (*Acts 23:12*). People hated him so much that sometimes whole troops of soldiers or even an entire army had to be called in to protect Paul from them.

As they were killing him, word reached the commander of the Roman garrison... When the mob saw the troops coming, they quit beating Paul...

As they reached the stairs, the mob grew so violent that the soldiers lifted Paul to their shoulders to protect him, and the crowd surged behind shouting, "Away with him, away with him!"

Acts 21: 31-32; 35-36

The... men were tugging at Paul... pulling him this way and that. Finally the commander, fearing they would tear him apart, ordered his soldiers to take him away.

Acts 23:10

The commander took the boy by the hand, and leading him aside asked, "What is it you want to tell me, lad?"

"Tomorrow," he told him, "the Jews are going to ask you to bring Paul before the Council again... But don't do it! There are more than forty men hiding along the road ready to jump him and kill him..."

Then the commander called two of his officers and ordered, "Get 200 soldiers ready to leave for Caesarea at nine o'clock tonight! Take 200 spearmen and 70 mounted cavalry. Give Paul a horse to ride and get him safely to Governor Felix."

Acts 23: 20-21; 23-24

What kind of a man needs to be protected by an escort of 200 soldiers, 70 horsemen and 200 spearmen? That's a 470-strong army for just one man! And they had to travel under cover of darkness, so grave was the threat posed by Paul's enemies. But why did they think it so important to kill him?

Paul wasn't the kind of man you could ignore. He "turned the world upside down" (*Acts 17:6*), preaching the gospel boldly and making deep inroads into the kingdom of darkness. Satan wanted to hinder Paul's ministry at all cost because this man was such a threat to his kingdom. So, he stirred up the Jews to oppose, persecute and try to kill Paul.

There was a time when Paul was sent to Italy to stand trial before the Roman Emperor. His crime? Doing the work of God! He set sail for Rome under the charge of a centurion named Julius but, several days into the voyage, the ship ran into rough weather. It became too dangerous to continue sailing, and Paul spoke to the officers about it.

"Sirs," he said, "I believe there is trouble ahead if we go on—perhaps shipwreck, loss of cargo, injuries and death." But the centurion didn't take Paul's advice seriously. Instead, he chose to listen to the ship's captain and the owner, who were all for carrying on with the voyage (*Acts 27:10-11*).

Thereafter, the storm grew worse. A wind of hurricane force caught the ship and blew it out to sea. As the waves rose higher, the crew threw the cargo and tackle overboard to lighten the ship. For many days, neither sun nor stars were visible as the raging storm continued to beat down on the ship. By then, everyone except Paul had lost all hope of being saved (there were 276 people on board). After they had gone a long time without food, Paul stood up in their midst and said:

"Men, you should have taken my advice not to sail from Crete; then you would have spared yourselves this damage and loss. But now I urge you to keep up your courage, because not one of you will be lost; only the ship will be destroyed.

"Last night an angel… said, 'Do not be afraid, Paul. You must stand trial before Caesar; and God has graciously given you the lives of all who sail with you.'"

Acts 27:21-24, NIV

Imagine a shipload of people as desperate and terrified as those men were! But what saved them was having a different thinker in their midst. Paul saw himself standing before Caesar when all the others saw themselves as food for the sea creatures. He saw Rome as his destination when they saw the sea as theirs. Now, that's a different thinker for you!

He saw life ahead and beyond the situation, while others saw only death. He saw a way out of their predicament when everyone else saw only a dead end. He took charge of the situation and gave them fresh hope when all their hope was gone. There was no other way out for them but to put their trust in the very man they hadn't wanted to listen to at first.

He was the only one on that ship who could save them because God had given all their lives into his hand. He was God's representative on that ship, and he had now become their leader. He even had to urge them to eat to keep up their strength—they had gone without food for two weeks because they had been too petrified with fear!

Soon after they had eaten, the ship struck a sandbar and ran aground. It began to break up and the soldiers decided to kill the prisoners to prevent them from escaping. But Julius stopped them because he wanted to save Paul. He couldn't afford to lose this man. In the crisis they were in— shipwrecked on an unknown shore—they needed someone like Paul. Someone with the benefit of divine guidance and counsel. Julius was blown away by how calm and composed this man was, when everyone else was in a frenzy of fear.

Paul had the mark of a true leader. He took charge when those who were supposed to be the leaders—the ship's captain, the crew, the centurion and the soldiers—cowered back in fear. When they were indecisive, he acted decisively. When they were losing their heads, his mind grew all the clearer. When their strength was all but gone, his increased. And this was his secret: he knew that God's strength was made perfect in his weakness (*2 Corinthians 12:9*). It was God's strength, not his, that carried him through.

The ship was wrecked, but all on board made it safely to shore. They soon learned that they were on the island of Malta. The local people welcomed them and built a bonfire on the beach to warm them up. Paul was helping to gather sticks for the fire when a viper crawled out and bit him.

The islanders waited for him to drop dead. "A murderer no doubt!" they concluded. "Though he has escaped the sea, justice will not permit him to live!" But when Paul remained unharmed after a long time, they changed their minds and decided he was a god (*Acts 28:4-6*). So, now that he had their attention and respect, Paul proceeded to hold a healing crusade on the island, and all the sick people were cured!

The islanders' initial perception of Paul was not unusual. Even today, anyone who is facing a string of challenges is commonly perceived to be under a curse of some kind—whether personal, family or generational. Wiseacres shake their heads and say, "He must have committed a terrible sin and brought down this retribution on himself" —much like what those people had said of Paul.

Some Christians go through life under the delusion that, as God's children, they would be protected from adversity and never have to face trials or tribulations of any kind at all.

And you wonder, whatever happened to suffering for the Lord? Or the testing of one's faith or development of one's character through trials?

> For to you it has been granted on behalf of Christ, not only to believe in Him, but also to suffer for His sake...
>
> *Philippians 1:29, NKJV*

> Consider it pure joy... whenever you face trials of many kinds, because you know that the testing of your faith produces perseverance. Let perseverance finish its work so that you may be mature and complete...
>
> *James 1:2-4, NIV*

> We can rejoice, too, when we run into problems and trials, for we know they are good for us—they help us learn to be patient. And patience develops strength of character in us and helps us trust God more... until finally our hope and faith are strong and steady.
>
> *Romans 5:3-4*

There was nothing wrong with Paul. He was simply suffering for the sake of Christ—persecuted for preaching the gospel. He was a righteous man, totally devoted to God. Yet he went through one terrible ordeal after another, of the kind most of us will only read about. Think about all that he suffered:

> "I have... been put in jail... often, been whipped times without number, and faced death again and again and again. Five different times the Jews gave me their terrible thirty-nine lashes. Three times I was beaten with rods. Once I was stoned. Three times I was shipwrecked. Once I was in the open sea all night and the whole next day.

"I have traveled many weary miles and have been often in great danger from flooded rivers and from robbers and from my own people, the Jews, as well as from the hands of the Gentiles. I have faced grave dangers from mobs in the cities and from death in the deserts and in the stormy seas and from men who claim to be brothers in Christ but are not.

"I have lived with weariness and pain and sleepless nights. Often I have been hungry and thirsty and have gone without food; often I have shivered with cold, without enough clothing to keep me warm."

2 Corinthians 11:23-27

Now, I am not saying that we should always expect the worst to happen to us or that we should passively accept the bad things that come to us. In fact, we should all pray for God's protection (*Psalm 91:1-7*), deliverance (*2 Thessalonians 3:2; 2 Corinthians 1:10-11*) and provision (*Philippians 4:19*). What I am saying here is that, as long as we live in this fallen world, we are not exempt from suffering. But the good news is that God is always with us, whatever we are going through: "for the eyes of the LORD range throughout the earth to strengthen those whose hearts are fully committed to him" (*2 Chronicles 16:9, NIV*).

One thing we need to understand is that, while God will *strengthen* us as we go through storms, He will not always deliver us from them. But, even if He doesn't deliver us, there is nothing wrong with Him—or with us. Remember what Shadrach, Meshach and Abednego said to King Nebuchadnezzar when he was about to throw them into the fiery furnace?

"God is able to deliver us," they told the king, "but even if He chooses not to, we will still be faithful to Him!" Their relationship with God wasn't founded only on benefits. It wasn't determined by circumstances. It was a relationship rooted in their unshakeable, unconditional faith in God.

When Jesus was going about His earthly ministry, many people followed Him only for the benefits He could give them. Some, because of His ability to multiply food; others, because they needed healing and nothing else. They were not interested in establishing a relationship with Him. But Paul, Daniel and those other guys—Shadrach, Meshach and Abednego—were ready to follow God in life *and in death*. That was why Paul said, "For to me, to live is Christ, and to die is gain" (*Philippians 1:21, NKJV*).

Seeing beyond death to the life beyond

Not long before Paul died, he wrote to Timothy, who was like a son to him. In his letter, he talked about his impending death at the hands of his executioners:

> As for me, my life has already been poured out as an offering to God. The time of my death is near.
>
> *2 Timothy 4:6, NLT*

Paul didn't live to a ripe old age and die a dignified death in bed. He died a gruesome death, martyred for his faith. But that doesn't mean there was something wrong with him or with God. Too often, people judge others by how they die. They point to random verses in the Bible—*Psalm 91:14-16,* for example—to support their belief that God will always protect the righteous and satisfy them with long life on earth. So, if someone dies an untimely death, they conclude that he couldn't have been righteous when he was alive.

Of course, God loves and honors His saints. But the truth is that He can decide to take us home any time and in any way He chooses. Going home to our Creator before our threescore and ten years are up (*Psalm 90:10*) doesn't mean our lives are being cut short because we have committed some terrible sin. Dying in an accident doesn't make us any less loved by God than if we had died of old age.

In fact, it doesn't matter what kind of death we die, because our bodies will all end up in the same place—the earth. This is because these physical bodies of ours are made of earthly material: "For you were made from the ground, and to the ground you will return" (*Genesis 3:19*).

But the real you—your spirit—will not die. Instead, you will leave this earth for your final destination. And whether this is going to be eternal life or everlasting punishment is determined, not by how you died, but by how you have lived your life. A dignified death will not increase anyone's chances of inheriting eternal life.

If people are judged by how they die, what about Jesus, our Lord and Savior? Wasn't His crucifixion one of the most shameful and painful ways anyone could die? In fact, many mocked Him as He hung dying on the cross—the passersby, chief priests, scribes and elders (*Matthew 27:39-43*).

Are we going to mock others because of how they died, the same way as those people mocked Jesus? The Word of God warns us against sitting in the seat of the scornful (*Psalm 1:1*). What is important is not the kind of death a person dies, whether he meets with a violent or peaceful end. What is important is the end result of his death. The death of Jesus resulted in our salvation. He went through every punishment for us to have abundant life.

And how about the apostles of Jesus Christ? If you are a limited thinker, you will be terribly discouraged to learn that most of them were brutally killed. They were either crucified, beheaded, stoned, speared or clubbed to death. When Jesus was still with them in the world, He had already warned them about the kind of death they would die:

> "Remember the word that I said to you, 'A servant is not greater than his master.' If they persecuted Me, they will also persecute you."
>
> *John 15:20, NKJV*

The apostles were fully prepared for the worst. A cruel death at the hands of their persecutors didn't come as a surprise to them. It didn't mean that they had lost; they knew it was to their gain, for eternal rewards awaited them. They had their minds set on things above (*Colossians 3:2*). They had their eyes fixed on the author and finisher of their faith (*Hebrews 12:2*). They saw beyond death to the eternal life that lay beyond the grave.

According to early Christian historians and writers, Peter was crucified. So was his brother Andrew as well as Simon the Zealot. When Peter was sentenced to be crucified, he felt himself to be unworthy of dying in the same manner as his Savior. So, at his own request, he was crucified upside down.

From all accounts, the other apostles suffered terribly too. Matthew and Thomas were impaled with spears. Matthias—who had been chosen to replace Judas Iscariot—was stoned to death, as was James Alpheus. James Zebedee was beheaded. His brother John survived several attempts on his life. Tertullian, an early Christian theologian, wrote that the Roman Emperor Domitian had the apostle dumped into a pot of boiling oil in front of a crowd of spectators.

Miraculously, John stood up in the pot, totally unharmed, and many of the spectators converted to Christianity because of this. Furious at this unexpected turn of events, Domitian had the apostle banished to the island of Patmos. It was there that John wrote the Book of Revelation.

Did God turn His back on the apostles? Didn't He love them? Or was John the only one He loved, that he alone was spared? The truth is that the apostles themselves never doubted God's love and faithfulness. They rejoiced that God had counted them worthy to suffer for Him (*Acts 5:40-41*). They rejoiced that they could share in the sufferings of Christ (*1 Peter 4:13*). They looked forward to receiving the crown of life from the Lord Himself (*Revelation 2:10*).

I don't know of any great man or woman of God whose life was smooth sailing all the way through. Look at all the most notable people in the Bible—Abraham, Isaac, Jacob, Joseph, Job, Moses, Ruth, David, Esther, Isaiah, Jeremiah, Daniel and his friends, Hosea, Mary the mother of Jesus, and John the Baptist are some of the names that come to mind. These people had their challenges, but they fought the good fight, ran their race, and left a heritage of faithfulness for the generations that came after them. Their life stories continue to inspire and encourage us to this very day.

Ask yourself, what is the testament you are leaving for those who come after you? Would they find you faithful? Would they learn anything of value from you if they were to observe how you handled trials that came your way? When we have the right attitude, we will be able to overcome any challenge with grace, composure and joy. We will put our enemies to shame and light the way for the generations that come after us.

Hope in hopeless situations

A different thinker sees hope in hopeless situations. He sees a promising outcome when the circumstances look totally unpromising to everyone else. He can see hope even in the face of death because he can see life beyond death. He can see the resurrection of what seems dead to others. He can see rebirth, revival, renewal and restoration in relationships and situations that have long been dead and buried.

When others have lost their hope, he sees a reason to go on hoping. This is because he knows the One in whom he has put his hope. He has good reason to hope because he knows that his Redeemer lives. He understands that the battle is not over yet. The world may say it's all over and done with. But he knows it isn't over until his God says so.

It's not over until God says so

Jesus loved Mary and Martha and their brother Lazarus. This was the Mary who had anointed Jesus with perfume and wiped His feet with her hair. But when the two sisters sent word to Jesus that Lazarus was very sick, "he stayed where he was for the next two days and made no move to go to them" (*John 11:6*).

It was only after those two days had passed and Lazarus was already dead that Jesus set off to visit them. By the time He arrived, Lazarus had already been buried for four days. When Martha met Him, the first thing she said to Him was that, if He had come earlier, Lazarus would not have died. The following conversation then took place between them:

Jesus said to her, "Your brother will rise again."
Martha said to Him, "I know that he will rise again in the resurrection at the last day."
John 11:23-24, NKJV

They were talking at cross-purposes here. Jesus was telling Martha that He was going to raise Lazarus from the dead that very day. But she thought He was talking about the resurrection of the dead on the Last Day. She couldn't imagine her brother rising up from his grave there and then.

She was used to dead people staying dead. That was the normal, usual way with dead people. They didn't simply rise up from their graves whenever they felt like it. She couldn't see that it was going to be any different in her brother's case. She couldn't see what Jesus saw. She couldn't believe what He was telling her. She was a limited thinker.

She was mourning the loss of her brother and thinking she would never see him alive again until the Last Day. Jesus had to make it clear to her that He was the Resurrection and the Life, and He could resurrect Lazarus any time He wanted.

> Jesus said to her, "I am the resurrection and the life. He who believes in Me, though he may die, he shall live. And whoever lives and believes in Me shall never die."
>
> *John 11:25-26, NKJV*

Mary was weeping, and so were the Jews who had come to offer their condolences to the sisters. Jesus wept when He saw their grief. But He wasn't weeping for the same reason that they were. He wasn't weeping because Lazarus was dead; He knew He could fix that. He was weeping because He felt their intense pain and loss.

Everyone believed that Jesus had come too late to save Lazarus. They said to one another, "If only He had come just a little bit earlier when Lazarus was still alive, He could have kept him from dying. But now that Lazarus is dead, even He can't do anything. Dead is dead!"

They believed Jesus could heal the sick because they had seen or heard of Him doing so. Some might even have believed He could bring the dead back to life—if the death had occurred only a short while ago, as in the case of Jairus' daughter (see *Mark 5:22-24, 35-43*). But Lazarus? He had been dead four days! They had already buried him, and now his body lay rotting in the tomb. There was no way a dead body in that condition could be resurrected! Or so they believed.

They thought Jesus had come just for the burial service and all He could do would be to offer His condolences to Martha and Mary. They believed it was all over with Lazarus; no longer could they count him among the living. But what they didn't know was that it wasn't over until Jesus said so. When He told them to remove the stone covering the grave, Martha protested, "Lord, by this time he stinks."

Jesus had to remind her of what He had told her earlier: "But didn't I tell you that you will see a wonderful miracle from God if you believe?" (*John 11:40*) And what a wonderful miracle it was!

> Jesus called in a loud voice, "Lazarus, come out!" The dead man came out, his hands and feet wrapped with strips of linen, and a cloth around his face.
>
> *John 11:43-44, NIV*

Jesus was a different thinker. He didn't listen to the crowd but only to His Father. The crowd had concluded that it was all over for Lazarus, but Jesus knew it wasn't over until God said so. And God had said otherwise: "This sickness will not end in death. No, it is for God's glory so that God's Son may be glorified through it" (*John 11:4, NIV*). Jesus saw life in the midst of and beyond death. He saw a resurrection that would glorify God and change the way we see death.

Changing the way we see death

You might be saying now, "Well, Jesus is God. Of course, He can bring the dead back to life. But you can't expect mere mortal men or women to be able to do that." If this is what you are thinking, then how do you explain the fact that Elijah, Elisha, Peter and Paul were able to raise the dead too?

The Bible tells us that Elijah was an ordinary man, just like any other man (*James 5:17*). But he was able to see life in the face of death. At the time our story begins, Elijah was staying with a widow who had been commanded by God to feed him. There was famine in the land, but God provided the widow with a continuous supply of food. Then one day the widow's only son fell sick and died. The woman was devastated but Elijah saw the situation differently.

> And he stretched himself out on the child three times, and cried out to the LORD and said, "O LORD my God, I pray, let this child's soul come back to him."
>
> Then the LORD heard the voice of Elijah; and the soul of the child came back to him, and he revived.
>
> *1 Kings 17:21-22, NKJV*

The boy came back to life because of a man who saw death differently. He saw life in this boy even when there was no life in him. He didn't panic but took control over the situation. He knew he could still plead with God for this child's life. He knew it was not over until God said so.

Elijah wasn't the only person to raise the dead to life. His protégé Elisha did the same too (*2 Kings 4:18-37*). So did Peter (see *Acts 9:36-43*) and Paul (see *Acts 20:7-12*). These people saw death differently from others. They saw life in the midst of death. So did Stephen, who saw heaven and a glorious life awaiting him beyond death.

The Bible describes Stephen as a man full of faith and the Holy Spirit (*Acts 6:5*). He did great miracles among the people. He spoke with such wisdom and power that his enemies were no match for him. So, sore losers that they were, they stirred up the people against him and dragged him before the Jewish Council on trumped-up charges.

When Stephen appeared before the Council, he took the opportunity to preach to the Jewish leaders there. But they resisted the Holy Spirit and were too stiff-necked to accept the truth:

> When they heard these things they were cut to the heart, and they gnashed at him with their teeth. But he, being full of the Holy Spirit, gazed into heaven and saw the glory of God, and Jesus standing at the right hand of God, and said, "Look! I see the heavens opened and the Son of Man standing at the right hand of God!"
>
> *Acts 7:54-56, NKJV*

Stephen's eyes were not on the persecutors surrounding him. No, he looked beyond and above them to heaven, where he saw the glory of God. When he told the Jews what he saw, they dragged him out of the city and stoned him:

> And as the murderous stones came hurtling at him, Stephen prayed, "Lord Jesus, receive my spirit." And he fell to his knees, shouting, "Lord, don't charge them with this sin!" and with that, he died.
>
> *Acts 7:59-60*

Stephen was a different thinker. He forgave the very people who were inflicting the most excruciating pain on him. He didn't carry any bitterness or hatred of them to his death.

Instead of seeing those stones hurtling at him, he saw the glory of God. Instead of seeing death, he saw a platform that would usher him into the presence of his heavenly Father. Instead of seeing the end of his life, he saw the beginning of his new life. He saw a better world than the one he was leaving behind. Like Paul, he could say, "For me, to live is Christ and to die is gain."

An ordinary thinker wouldn't have been able to handle the situation the way Stephen did. Ordinary thinkers see death as a great loss and the end of everything for them. But a different thinker sees death, not as the end, but as the beginning of the real and glorious life he would have with his Maker. This is why many men and women of God have died for their faith. They had the opportunity to deny their God and live, but they didn't take that path. They chose to die a martyr's death because they saw a different reality.

Seeing life in death doesn't apply only to the death of our bodies but to any other kind of death as well—dying marriages, dead relationships, dead-end careers and dead-broke financial situations, for example. But this different way of seeing doesn't come easily. You have to make a clear, firm decision that this is what you want and you are going to work very hard to achieve it. You are going to develop the ability to see and get what you want out of any situation, no matter how hopeless it looks. You are going to see solutions in challenges, hope in hopeless situations, and life in the midst of death. You are going to give yourself a chance.

CHAPTER 4

Celebrates Victory Before It Manifests

A DIFFERENT THINKER CREATES AND CELEBRATES VICTORY within himself before the victory manifests itself outwardly. He sees success in the spiritual realm with his spiritual eyes before his physical eyes can see it. He sees victory before he starts a project. He knows the onus lies on him to create within himself the victory he wants to see, so that this victory can then be birthed into the physical realm.

This means he can experience victory within himself long before any evidence of this victory shows up on the outside. This makes him see himself as a victor even in the face of setbacks or apparent defeat—and, seeing himself as a victor, he begins to celebrate victory before any sign of it is evident to others. This is the secret to his success.

His success journey starts and ends with *celebration*. He is able to celebrate success even at the conception stage of an endeavor because he acknowledges God's help right from the start. He continues to celebrate each step of the way, even as he faces and overcomes obstacles in his path. He does it all with joy, encouraged by what he has achieved at each stage. This attitude of joy impels him to press on towards his goal. And, because he knows he has God's help, he has reason to celebrate even before he has completed his journey.

A different thinker counts every blessing. He doesn't celebrate only the big and obvious successes. He understands that small successes are his stepping stones to greater ones.

He doesn't despise small beginnings; he knows they are the foundation stones upon which the biggest buildings are established. He knows that every brick is important in the construction of a house; therefore, he doesn't take anything for granted. This is why he celebrates every step of the way.

He celebrates the small steps he takes today because what he learns today will make his tomorrow better. His eyes are not only on the future but the present as well. He can't afford to miss the action today, because he knows what he does today will shape his tomorrow for better or for worse.

He celebrates a win on the inside even while he is still fighting on the outside. This gives him the strength to fight harder. He celebrates within himself because he knows he needs to be a victor on the inside before he can win on the outside. He realizes that, when he is defeated inside, he is defeated on the outside too. When he feels good inside, he will feel good outside. He becomes who he thinks he is.

Our actions reveal how we feel inside. How we carry ourselves reveals how we see ourselves. When you are standing up on the inside, you won't be easily put down by whatever is outside you. When you are confident and courageous inside, you become unstoppable on the outside. You can't be strong inside and still be weak outwardly. This is because the inner person is stronger than the outward self and influences what you do on the outside.

We can be strong on the inside because the Word of God tells us that in every situation we are more than conquerors through Him who loves us (*Romans 8:37*). We know that God is working all things together for our good (*Romans 8:28*). Therefore, we have every reason to celebrate victory even in the midst of a crisis. We can celebrate victory even in the face of what seems to be impending disaster or defeat.

Our understanding of God's Word and of His power is the reason we can rejoice and laugh in situations that would have made others cry. We live and walk by faith in God and not by what we see in the world around us. And because we see through spiritual eyes of faith, we are not easily moved by what is visibly happening in the physical world. We know that things are not always what they seem to be.

We walk in the spirit—and the spirit in us, being fully alive and active, sees victory in the spiritual realm and celebrates it. This victory is real, even though the situation may still be looking hopeless in the physical realm. But it is the spiritual that prevails over the physical; and the victory that we have seen first in the spirit will in good time manifest itself in the physical world.

Celebrate victory and leave everything else to God

Remember the story of Mary in Chapter 2? The young girl who was told by an angel that she would give birth to the Son of God *while she was still a virgin... and still single?* (She was engaged to Joseph at the time, but they weren't married yet). So, what did she do after receiving such extraordinary news? She celebrated!

She praised and worshipped God. She acknowledged the plan of God and celebrated victory before she was even pregnant. She celebrated even though she knew that having a baby out of wedlock would expose her to public disgrace— and most likely stoning as well. She celebrated even though she wasn't sure what Joseph's reaction would be, when the baby wasn't from him. She celebrated in a situation that would have left most people in confusion, doubt and fear.

Mary didn't waste her time dwelling on the problems she was likely to face because of the situation she was in.

She didn't waste her breath on questions she didn't have answers for. She focused on the good news she had been told, and she left everything else to God. She knew He would be faithful to bring to completion what He had promised her. She had no room in her heart for misery or worry but only for celebration of the victory she knew would one day be manifested for all to see.

Creating an atmosphere of victory

> At dawn of the seventh day they started out again, but this time they went around the city not once, but seven times. The seventh time, as the priests blew a long, loud trumpet blast, Joshua yelled to the people, "*Shout!* The Lord has given us the city!"
>
> So when the people heard the trumpet blast, they shouted as loud as they could. And suddenly the walls of Jericho crumbled and fell before them, and the people of Israel poured into the city from every side and captured it!
>
> *Joshua 6: 15-16, 20*

The Israelites celebrated the fall of Jericho before it actually happened. They blew trumpets and gave a loud shout of victory—and, following that, the walls of Jericho fell before their eyes. God had already told them He was giving them the city, but they too had a part to play to make it happen. They needed to create an atmosphere of victory first. Their celebration of victory paved the way for the actual victory to take place.

They didn't say, "Let us wait and see what happens first, and then we will celebrate." They didn't wait for the walls to fall down first before deeming it appropriate to celebrate.

In the natural order of things, we want to see results first before we will celebrate. No results, no celebration. But those people did it the other way round. They did not conform to the norm; they simply did what God told them to do.

No one can create an atmosphere of victory for you. It is your responsibility to do it for yourself. When you celebrate victory before it materializes, you are creating a platform for that victory to show up in the physical realm. You are paving the way for the actual victory to happen. You are proclaiming your faith in God.

Celebrate your healing even while you are still in pain, because you believe you have been healed by Jesus' stripes. Celebrate the book you are writing even before you have it published, because you believe it will be of help to readers. Whatever you set out to do, celebrate victory whilst still in the midst of struggles. Celebration lifts up the spirit; it gives you the joy and strength to press on and not give up.

Why would you continue to do something if you don't believe you will one day succeed at it? Celebrating success before it materializes signifies that you believe in what you are doing. If you can't celebrate, perhaps it is because you don't really believe that what you are doing is of any value. Celebration is an acknowledgment that what you are doing is too important to fail—and that you have the God-given talents, intelligence and creativity to make a success of it.

Celebrating in the midst of trials

James 1:2-3 tells us to count it all joy when we face trials of many kinds because the testing of our faith produces patience. In other words, we can celebrate in the midst of trials because these trials are for our benefit; they are put there to help produce patience in us and build character.

Then be happy, for when the way is rough, your patience has a chance to grow. So let it grow, and don't try to squirm out of your problems. For when your patience is finally in full bloom, then you will be ready for anything, strong in character, full and complete.

James 1:3-4

It is possible for us to keep our joy, no matter what life throws at us. This is because staying joyful is a conscious decision we make and act upon. We need to understand that we alone are responsible for our own happiness. We alone decide if we want to let circumstances or other people rob us of our joy.

Terrible times may come, when we can't help but cry our hearts out. It is alright to cry; nothing wrong with having a good cry. It is wrong only when we do it out of a lack of faith and when it keeps us from moving forward. You can cry for a season, but then you have to move on. If you keep wallowing in your grief, you will miss out on the joys God has in store for you. Those joys will surely come, because the Word of God assures us that weeping only lasts for a night but joy comes in the morning (*Psalm 30:5*).

The God who came to our help in the past can be trusted to do so again. We may not know how or when, but we know He will save us yet again. We recall how He has helped us before; how we escaped as a bird from the fowlers' snare. The snare broke and we escaped (*Psalm 124:7*). We recall how He made a way through the sea (*Isaiah 43:16*); how He made a way for us where there was no way. As we recall God's faithfulness, we know we can leave everything in His hands. He will do a new thing for us; He will make a way in the wilderness (*Isaiah 43:19*). He will make a way out for us.

We can keep our joy and peace even when tough times leave us weak and helpless. We can celebrate, knowing that God's strength takes over when our own strength fails—for we know that His strength is made perfect in our weakness (*2 Corinthians 12:9*). We can rejoice because our everlasting God neither faints nor grows weary. He gives power to the weary and strength to the weak (*Isaiah 40:28-29*). He gives sleep to us, His beloved (*Psalm 127:2*), when the storms of life are raging about us. We can choose to enjoy a peaceful rest and let Him take care of the storms for us.

Peace in the storm

> As evening fell, Jesus said to his disciples, "Let's cross to the other side of the lake." So they took him just as he was and started out... But soon a terrible storm arose. High waves began to break into the boat until it was nearly full of water and about to sink.
>
> Jesus was asleep at the back of the boat with his head on a cushion. Frantically they wakened him, shouting, "Teacher, don't you even care that we are all about to drown?"
>
> *Mark 4:35-38*

The disciples couldn't believe their eyes! Here they were, tossed about by high waves that were even now crashing into the boat and rapidly filling it with water. And there was Jesus, fast asleep, oblivious to the racket going on around Him— the raging storm, wildly pitching boat and disciples' frenzied shouting. Worse still, He showed no sign of waking up any time soon. How could anyone go on sleeping, when the boat was full of water! It made no sense at all. They decided they had better wake Him up... before they all drowned.

Then he rebuked the wind and said to the sea, "Quiet down!" And the wind fell, and there was a great calm!

And he asked them, "Why were you so fearful? Don't you even yet have confidence in me?"

And they were filled with awe and said among themselves, "Who is this man, that even the winds and seas obey him?"

Mark 4:39-41

The disciples had been with Jesus for some time now. They had seen Him do many miracles[2] but they still hadn't caught on to who He was and what He was trying to teach them. Of course, the main reason Jesus came to earth was to shed His blood and die so that mankind might be saved. But He also came to show us the way. He came to show us how we are to live our lives in Him. But it looked like those disciples just couldn't get it, even though they were always with Him.

They weren't putting into practice what He had been trying to teach them. They were still so fearful, so lacking in faith. He wanted them to understand who He really was, and the kind of power and authority He had. He wanted them to understand the kind of God they were serving and the kind of life they were called to lead. He wanted them to understand the power and authority they could have, if only they believed—power and authority over every situation, even the fiercest storm.

He wanted and expected them, after all that time spent with Him, to have a different mindset from the common run of men, a different approach to challenges; to stay strong and serene when the storms of life were raging about them.

---

[2] To find out some of the miracles Jesus had done up to this point in time, see *John 2:1-12; 4:46-54; 5:1-15; Matthew 4:23-25; 8:14-15; 9:1-8; 12:9-14; Mark 1:21-31; 40-45; Luke 7:11-17.*

He wanted them to be in control of situations and not let situations control them. He wanted them to learn that, no matter how severe the storm, it would soon blow over. All would be well again. Storms never last forever.

He wanted them to be calm and composed in the face of challenges, because they were leaders who would one day continue His work on earth. That day was fast approaching, when He would have to leave them and return to the Father. He wanted them to be able to weather all kinds of storms because they were going to meet many of those, when they were out there ministering to people. He didn't want them to freak out every time they ran into persecution or problems.

He wanted leaders who lived and led by example; solution providers whom others could look to for help. They had to fully understand that faith was the main ingredient needed for success in ministry and mission work. They needed faith to perform miracles.

The truth is, we don't lose anything by keeping our cool. In fact, a peaceful mind helps us handle situations better. On the other hand, we stand to lose everything if we panic, since this means we won't be able to think straight or make the best decisions. Most storms in life will blow over sooner or later but, because of such temporary storms, we tend to make rash decisions—often with lifelong consequences.

Many of us mismanage our emotions when trials come our way. We get miserable and angry. We pull a long face. We whine and complain, often loudly. We make sure that everyone in the neighborhood knows we are going through a hard time. We behave as if it's everyone's fault that we are suffering, and we forget that others have their own share of trouble too. Pandering to our feelings in this way doesn't solve any problem. It may even aggravate our problems.

Praise in prison

There was once a slave girl who could tell people's fortunes because of a demon in her. One day she met the apostle Paul, who cast the demon out of her. Of course, that angered her masters as they could no longer make money off her fortune-telling! So, they dragged Paul and his companion Silas to court on false charges and incited the people against them:

> The crowd joined in the attack against Paul and Silas, and the magistrates ordered them to be stripped and beaten with rods. After they had been severely flogged, they were thrown into prison, and the jailer was commanded to guard them carefully. When he received these orders, he put them in the inner cell and fastened their feet in the stocks.
>
> About midnight Paul and Silas were praying and singing hymns to God, and the other prisoners were listening to them.
>
> *Acts 16:22-25, NIV*

Paul and Silas handled the situation differently from how others would have done. They had been cruelly beaten and then thrown into a maximum-security prison. And all for doing the work of God; not because they had committed any crime. There they were in that dungeon, in great pain after being severely flogged, and virtually immobilized with their feet clamped into the stocks. So, what did they do?

They sang praises to God! Strange behavior indeed! In the midst of their suffering, they saw a need and a reason to praise God. They saw a reason not to let circumstances rob them of their joy. They saw a reason to celebrate victory when there seemed to be no way they could win in this case.

They kept their joy and composure because they knew that God was able to do exceedingly abundantly above all they could ask or think. Though they were in a terrible situation, they had a reason to celebrate, because they had been given the gift of life. They had been beaten and jailed, but their lives were spared. They were still alive, and now they saw an opportunity to bring the gospel to the other prisoners.

They were in prison, but they were not imprisoned. They were physically confined, but their spirits were free. They still had direct access to the omnipresent God. They still had access to the Holy Spirit's help and comfort. They had all the freedom to praise God, and praise God they did— not just quietly by themselves but openly, so that the other prisoners could hear them loud and clear. And, as they continued to worship God, this was what happened:

> Suddenly there was a great earthquake; the prison was shaken to its foundations, all the doors flew open—and the chains of every prisoner fell off!
>
> *Acts 16:26*

Isn't this amazing? Isn't this what's meant for those who have chosen to praise God in the midst of their pain? People thought they had finally got those two men locked up and put away. But no one can lock you up or put you away when God wants to set you free—even if it takes Him an earthquake to do it. Paul and Silas were delivered out of that prison because they celebrated victory before it actually happened.

Of course, this doesn't mean that God is going to stage a jailbreak every time someone in prison celebrates and sings praises to Him. Celebration will invariably bring victory, but that victory can take many forms. Most times in fact, God chose not to deliver Paul when he was thrown into prison.

You can even say that Paul was a "regular" in prison, since he was incarcerated so often that it looked like he was practically living there! But Paul didn't see prison the way others saw it, as a setback in life. He had learnt to make the best of every situation. He had learnt the secret of being content in any and every situation (*Philippians 4:12*).

Paul was frequently imprisoned without just cause, but he didn't waste his time weeping or indulging in self-pity. He had learnt to benefit from all that was meant to break him. He saw his imprisonment as an opportunity to write freely, without distractions from people or the demands of his apostolic ministry. Four of his Epistles—Ephesians, Philippians, Colossians and Philemon—were written when he was in prison.

Different thinking is being able to see light in the midst of and beyond darkness. It is being able to create the light you want to see, even when you are still in gross darkness. It is knowing you have the ability to create this light because you are a creator: because you take after your Creator, who has made you in His image and likeness (*Genesis 1:27*).

In the beginning, there was only darkness. Then God said, "Let there be light." And light appeared (*Genesis 1:3*). God called the light out of the darkness. He called into being things that did not exist at first (*Romans 4:17*). Different thinking is learning to do the same: to call into being things that did not exist at first. And that is faith.

Getting back what you have lost

Different thinking is also being able to see things that have been lost or stolen restored. There was a time when Elisha, together with a company of prophets, decided to build a bigger house that could comfortably accommodate them all.

They went to the Jordan River and began cutting down some of the trees there. But, as one of them was chopping, his axe head fell into the water. Observe what happened next:

> "Oh, sir," he cried, "it was borrowed!"
>
> "Where did it fall?" the prophet asked. The youth showed him the place, and Elisha cut a stick and threw it into the water; and the axe head rose to the surface and floated! "Grab it," Elisha said to him; and he did.
>
> *2 Kings 6:5-7*

A solid iron axe head floating on the water? It was out of this world! It happened only because a different thinker believed that iron could float—and he got what he believed! He didn't panic or lose hope when the axe head sank to the bottom of the river. He saw the possibility of getting back what was lost.

That school of prophets was under Elisha's leadership, and he was giving his students an object lesson on believing in the impossible. He had to set the standard; otherwise, what were they going to learn from him, if he thought the same way they did? He had to show them a whole new way of thinking that was poles apart from what they were used to. He had to show them the way of the different thinker.

A different thinker has a way of seeing lost things restored and broken things mended. He can see reconciliation for broken relationships and restoration for the years that the locusts have eaten (*Joel 2:25*). Nothing is impossible with him, because he has trained his mind to think this way.

He always expects the extraordinary to happen, and he will not be disappointed. Things may not always happen the same way. The axe head may not always float; it may be restored in a novel and even more amazing way—because God is always doing new things (*Isaiah 43:19*).

Creating a platform for miracles

A different thinker creates an atmosphere for miracles. He knows that things don't just happen by chance, so he creates a platform for God to do His work. Remember when Jesus fed thousands of people from the little food that was all they had then? He told the people to sit down. He did this even when there was no sign that the food was going to be multiplied. He created a platform for a miracle to take place, and God never disappoints when He sees such acts of faith.

To create a platform where God can work, we need only to have faith in Him. When Lazarus died, his sisters didn't believe he could come back to life again (*John 11:21-32*). Because of their unbelief, they didn't prepare any platform for a miracle to take place. They didn't believe their brother could rise again, except on the Last Day.

Do you know what Jesus said to them? "Only believe, and you will see the glory of God." Isn't that beautiful? *Only believe.* If only we believe, we can see miracles. Creating an atmosphere for miracles is simply inviting God to come and visit earth. It is permitting Him to do what He knows is best for us.

If only we believe, we can create a platform where heaven meets earth to produce supernatural results. We can bring the kingdom of God to earth, because we have been given the keys of the kingdom of heaven. Whatever we bind on earth will be bound in heaven, and whatever we loose on earth will be loosed in heaven (see *Matthew 16:19*). The prophet Elijah understood very well the kind of power this gives us. He held the keys of the kingdom of heaven and locked up the rain for three and a half years. He went away with the keys, and it didn't rain again until he said so.

> Elijah was as completely human as we are, and yet when he prayed earnestly that no rain would fall, none fell for the next three and a half years! Then he prayed again, this time that it would rain, and down it poured...
>
> *James 5:17-18*

Elijah knew who he was and his position and purpose in God. He knew the kind of God he lived for and served. This was what made him stand out from the rest of humanity. This is what made him a different and exceptional thinker. This was what gave him power, authority and control over kings, kingdoms and situations. This was what made him a great prophet and history maker.

A different thinker takes God at His word when He says, "Ask, and it will be given to you" (*Matthew 7:7*). This gives him the confidence that, when he invites God to come and visit earth and show forth His glory, he will be given exactly what he has asked for. He knows that, by creating this platform for God to work on, his miracle is on the way.

A rare touch of faith

She was so tired of it all... tired of the long years of pain... tired of the constant bleeding... tired of people shunning her, treating her as an outcast because of her ailment. After twelve years of running all over the place, trying to find a cure, she had given up on all those physicians who had sucked her dry of her money... but still couldn't heal her. In fact, she had only got worse from their ministrations.

Then she started hearing news of a Great Physician who could heal every kind of sickness. What's more, He had just come to her hometown and even now crowds of people were out there on the streets, following Him wherever He went.

"If I only touch His cloak, I will be healed," she said to herself. And she did just that. She came up behind Jesus and touched the hem of His cloak. She created a platform to receive the healing she wanted from God—and at once her bleeding stopped.

The street was jam-packed with people crowding and pressing against Jesus, and many were touching Him. But this woman's touch was different. This was a touch of faith. This was a touch that created an atmosphere for a miracle to happen. This was a touch that Jesus noticed right away:

> "Who touched me?" Jesus asked.
>
> When they all denied it, Peter said, "Master, the people are crowding and pressing against you."
>
> But Jesus said, "Someone touched me; I know that power has gone out from me."
>
> *Luke 8:45-46, NIV*

Jesus' question made no sense to His disciples. With such a large crowd jostling around Him, there would have been countless people touching Him! But one touch was different from the rest. One touch was unique. One touch alone drew the power out from Jesus. This woman touched Him with everything she had. She was determined to get her miracle. It was a touch of total faith, and Jesus knew it.

> Then the woman, seeing that she could not go unnoticed, came trembling and fell at his feet. In the presence of all the people, she told why she had touched him and how she had been instantly healed.
>
> Then he said to her, "Daughter, your faith has healed you. Go in peace."
>
> *Luke 8:47-48, NIV*

Mustard seed faith

One thing that greatly annoyed Jesus was the people's lack of faith. He even called His disciples, "you stubborn, faithless people!" (*Matthew 17:17*) because they were so short on faith. This was after they had failed to heal an epileptic boy. Jesus quickly rebuked the demon that was in the boy, and it left him at once (*Matthew 17:18*).

> Afterwards the disciples asked Jesus privately, "Why couldn't we cast that demon out?"
>
> "Because of your little faith," Jesus told them. "For if you had faith even as small as a tiny mustard seed, you could say to this mountain, 'Move!' and it would go far away. Nothing would be impossible."
>
> *Matthew 17:19-20*

If you had faith as small as a mustard seed. Isn't it wonderful that God honors even the littlest bit of faith? With faith the size of a mustard seed, you can move mountains. Nothing will be impossible for you. Jesus is always pleased when people have faith in God, and He often congratulated them for it when He was on earth. He always made it clear to them that they received their miracle because of their faith[3].

He wanted them to understand that they had a major role to play if they wanted Him to help them. They had only to believe in Him; by doing so, they were creating a platform from which He could intervene and operate on their behalf.

---

[3] Apart from the woman who was healed when she touched the hem of His coat (*Luke 8:43-48*), Jesus also commended several others for their faith. Among them were the centurion who believed that Jesus could heal his servant from afar by just speaking the word (*Matthew 8:5-13*); blind Bartimaeus, who shouted all the louder for Jesus when told by the crowd to shut up (*Mark 10:46-52*); the persistent Canaanite woman who sought healing for her demon-possessed daughter (*Matthew 15:22-28*); and the Samaritan leper who came back to thank Jesus (*Luke 17:11-19*).

That is how seriously He takes our faith. Faith has a way of attracting His attention, of compelling Him to attend to us. It is the language He fully understands. In fact, the Word of God goes so far as to say that "without faith, it is impossible to please God" (*Hebrews 11:6, NIV*). Without faith, we can't expect anything from God; lack of faith ties His hands.

When the woman touched the hem of Jesus' cloak and was cured, there were probably many other sick people in the crowd hoping to get healed too. But they didn't get their miracle—because they hadn't created a platform for it to happen. They didn't do anything to catch the attention of Jesus, like this woman did. They didn't go all out to get the help they wanted.

They were just milling around in the crowd, thinking to themselves: "Whatever will be, will be. If I don't get help, it just means that it wasn't meant to be. Whether I'm healed or not, there's nothing I can do about it." Now, the truth is that statements like these most often stem from a lack of faith—and they get you nowhere.

Undeniably, we don't always get what we want from God. For reasons best known to Him, He may not give us all that we want, at the time we want it. Nevertheless, the right thing to do is always to have faith. Whether I receive what I want from God or not, what is more important is that I have pleased Him with my faith; I did what I needed to do.

It has been said that God may respond to our prayers in one of three ways: *yes, no,* or *wait.* But people don't always understand Him. Every time we don't get exactly what we ask for, we conclude that God hasn't answered our prayers. We aren't able to think or see beyond what *we* want. It never occurs to us that maybe He wants us to wait on Him awhile.

Maybe He wants to give us something different, something better than what we have asked for. But the problem is that we want what we want, exactly as we want it, at the time we want it. We aren't interested in getting anything different.

This is one reason why people get disappointed with God. They fail to understand that what they want may not always turn out for their good. They fail to comprehend that God knows—much more than they do themselves—what is best for them. They think God should always dance to their tune each time they snap their fingers. But, if they could see into tomorrow, they would be singing a different tune now.

We are such inconsistent creatures. We think we want something but sooner or later we realize this is not what we actually want, it's something else… only for that "something else" to be eventually discarded too. This is why some people keep changing their spouses, relationships, careers or just about anything else. It is because they don't fully understand themselves. They don't know what they really want in life. Some just want whatever they see others flaunting, even though they don't genuinely need those things themselves.

But God understands us best because He is our Maker. He fully understands our nature. He sees into the depths of the human heart, with all its unspoken dreams and desires. He sees into the future. This is why we can totally trust Him to give us His best. If we don't get what we asked for, or we get something different instead, we can be sure that the thing we asked for was actually a bad idea in the first place —and what we have received is in fact truly the best for us.

> Because the foolishness of God is wiser than men, and the weakness of God is stronger than men.
>
> *1 Corinthians 1:25, NKJV*

Flexibility with God

People are easily deceived by outward appearances. Many have messed up their lives because they prioritized short-term gain over long-term benefits. The sad part about all this is that we do actually have the capability to make responsible decisions, if we set our minds to it. God in fact trusts us to do so and to handle the affairs of life wisely and well. But it was never His intention for us to do it all on our own, independently of Him.

We are a team with God; together with Him, we can achieve much more than if we were to go it alone. We really do need to involve God in every area of our lives—and to willingly accept whatever He gives us. It is important for us to keep an open mind when God gives us something different from what we asked for. Even when we have fully convinced ourselves that the things we want are what we need, we should be flexible and accept whatever God gives us instead; it might turn out to be better than what we asked for!

Flexibility with God leaves room for Him to do what He knows is best for you. The Bible tells us to trust in the Lord with all our heart and not to rely on our own understanding or think too highly of our own wisdom (*Proverbs 3:5-7*). Being flexible with God is not a sign of lack of faith; rather, it demonstrates your complete faith in Him. It shows that you are acknowledging His lordship over your life.

Flexibility with God is particularly important when it comes to making major decisions. Start by being upfront with God and telling Him: "Lord, I am asking for this, and I want it to be this way." There is nothing wrong with wanting what you want, your way, and telling Him that you want it exactly that way. He will decide if what you want is best for you or not, and this will determine the answer He gives you.

Now, after telling God what you would like Him to do for you, conclude your prayer by saying something like this: "This is what I want, Lord; but let your will be done in this, though." Say this even when you are very sure that you are asking Him for the "right" thing in the "right" way. This is being flexible with God and showing complete faith in Him.

Certainly, praying in this way is often easier said than done, especially when you are asking for things close to your heart and when everything is at stake. I am not talking here about glibly saying, "Your will be done" when your situation is at least bearable and you still have other options open to you. I am talking about saying it when you have run out of options and reached a dead end.

I am talking about the times when you are in tears because your situation is as painful and as bad as it can get, but you still go ahead and say this anyway:

> *Lord, this is what I seriously want and I am convinced that it's the right thing for me. But, regardless of what I need and how much I need this, I am open and flexible to whatever you decide is best for me. And I even prefer your will over mine, because I know your will is always perfect. I trust and accept your decision in this matter.*

This kind of prayer keeps bitterness away from you when you don't receive what you want from God. You are telling Him that, in spite of not getting what you asked for, you are still trusting Him to take control of your situation and to handle it better than what you thought was best. Even our Lord Jesus prayed in this way when the time came for Him to die a very painful death. He was open, honest and flexible with God, in spite of the agony He was in.

"Yet not my will, but yours be done"

This was how Jesus prayed to His Father, there in the Garden of Gethsemane:

> "Father, if you are willing, take this cup from me; yet not my will, but yours be done."
>
> *Luke 22:42, NIV*

Of course, Jesus knew God's will for Him. He knew He had been sent to earth to die for the sins of mankind. But the ordeal He was about to undergo would be beyond unbearable —which was why He asked for the cup of suffering to be taken from Him, if it was at all possible. Yet, having said that, He allowed God's will to be done in His life. His anguish didn't blind Him to God's bigger plan for humanity.

Jesus was praying the same kind of prayer that He had taught His disciples previously, while He was with them. This was how He had instructed them to pray:

> "This, then, is how you should pray:
>
> "'Our Father in heaven, hallowed be your name, your kingdom come, your will be done on earth as it is in heaven...'"
>
> *Matthew 6:9-10, NIV*

This prayer isn't only about God's will being done on earth; it is also about His will being done in our lives. The truth is that, when the will of God is fully done in our lives, it will inevitably be done on earth too. This is because we are the ones ruling and controlling the earth. We have been given dominion over the earth (*Genesis 1:28*). The state of our planet depends on our state as human beings. Earth is dependent on us. It becomes what *we* want it to become.

If our Lord Jesus thought it important to ask for His Father's will to take precedence in His life, who are we to pray otherwise? In fact, it is to our benefit to prefer God's will over our own. As I said earlier in this chapter, we don't always know what we really want or what is best for us. How then are we to pray, if we don't even know what to pray for? But, when we align ourselves with God's will, we will want what He wants, and His Spirit prays in and for us:

> In the same way, the Spirit helps us in our weakness. We do not know what we ought to pray for, but the Spirit himself intercedes for us through wordless groans.
>
> And he who searches our hearts knows the mind of the Spirit, because the Spirit intercedes for God's people in accordance with the will of God.
>
> *Romans 8:26-27, NIV*

When you give precedence to God's will, you will never be the same again. Everything about you becomes different. You see yourself differently. You see God differently. You understand Him and His Word differently. You think differently. You become an exceptional thinker and doer.

Conversely, when you choose your own will over God's, you are choosing limitation, which is the enemy of different thinking. You are consigning yourself to a purposeless life lived outside of the destiny God planned for you. You might even find yourself praying against His will without being aware of it. Of course, that's not going to get you anywhere:

> You ask and do not receive, because you ask amiss, that you may spend it on your pleasures.
>
> *James 4:3, NKJV*

Sometimes we don't receive what we ask for because our motives are all wrong. Something is just not right about our request, but we may not even be aware that we are asking wrongly. This is why we should always let God do whatever He wills in our lives. He always has the right motives.

God encourages you to take delight in Him; and, if you do, He says that He will give you the desires of your heart (*Psalm 37:4*). When you take delight in God wholeheartedly, it follows that you will also take delight in His will for you. All that He desires as His will for you become the desires of your heart too; and, as you pray to Him for those desires, He will give them to you because you are praying according to His will for you.

The same goes for all that you plan to do. The Bible exhorts us to commit everything we do to God:

> Roll your works upon the Lord [commit and trust them wholly to Him; He will cause your thoughts to become agreeable to His will, and] so shall your plans be established and succeed.
>
> *Proverbs 16:3, AMPC*

When you involve God fully in your life and commit all that you do to Him, He will bring your thoughts and plans into alignment with His will for you. You will not live or walk in confusion, but you will know He is guiding you because His Spirit will bear witness with your spirit that He is with you. And you will succeed in whatever you set out to do, because it is God Himself who establishes your plans for you.

The only time we shouldn't be flexible in prayer is when we are dealing with our enemy the devil. When we are engaging in spiritual warfare with the devil, we should know beyond any doubt that it is always God's will for us to win.

Have nothing to do with the evil one or his schemes. He is the deceiver of the whole world (*Revelation 12:9*). He is going all out to destroy you; there's no way you can afford to be flexible with him. Just give the command for him to be defeated. This is one of those times when you can be fully confident that you are praying according to God's will.

> This is the confidence we have in approaching God: that if we ask anything according to his will, he hears us. And if we know that he hears us—whatever we ask—we know that we have what we asked of him.
>
> *1 John 5:14-15, NIV*

When you know and understand God's will for you, and you are confident that you are praying in line with it, you can ask for what you want, and He will answer you accordingly.

Bending the rules in your favor

> A Canaanite woman... came to him, crying out, "Lord, Son of David, have mercy on me! My daughter is demon-possessed and suffering terribly."
>
> Jesus did not answer a word. So his disciples came to him and urged him, "Send her away, for she keeps crying out after us."
>
> He answered, "I was sent only to the lost sheep of Israel."
>
> The woman came and knelt before him. "Lord, help me!" she said.
>
> He replied, "It is not right to take the children's bread and toss it to the dogs."
>
> "Yes, it is, Lord," she said. "Even the dogs eat the crumbs that fall from their master's table."

Then Jesus said to her, "Woman, you have great faith! Your request is granted." And her daughter was healed at that moment.

Matthew 15:21-28, NIV

This poor woman came to Jesus with a desperate plea: "My daughter is suffering terribly, please save her." But Jesus turned down her request, and this was the reason He gave: "I was sent only to the lost sheep of Israel." In other words, she simply didn't qualify because she wasn't an Israelite.

Now, don't you find that strange? Was Jesus sent only to save the Jews? Obviously not. He was sent to save all of humanity—Jews and Gentiles alike. So, why did He give the woman such a reply? Possibly to test her; He wanted to see what her response would be. He saw something different in her, and He wanted to draw it out. And He succeeded.

Her request was rejected, but she stood her ground. She prepared a platform that Jesus couldn't resist but had to act upon. When He told her that He couldn't take "the children's bread" (the good things meant for the Israelites) and throw it to the dogs (outsiders like her), she didn't take offence.

Instead, she neatly turned the tables on Him—by using His own metaphor against Him. She said, "Yes, but the dogs are allowed to eat the crumbs, and all I want is a crumb!" She knew how to get around Him. If He refused to give her the bread, she knew how to be flexible and ask for the crumbs! He couldn't refuse her that!

She had already made up her mind that she was going to come out of that place with her miracle, and she prepared a platform that even God couldn't get off—not until He had given her what she wanted. Others in her place would have given up and walked away after being turned down by Jesus.

But not her. She was a different thinker. The rules might say that she didn't qualify for a miracle, but she believed that rules could be bent. Certainly, no rule was going to stop her from getting her daughter healed!

Speaking of rules, there was a time when Jesus was passing through Samaria and stopped to rest at Jacob's well. A Samaritan woman came to draw water from the well, and Jesus asked her for a drink. But the woman at first refused[4], because the rule was that Jews and Samaritans were not supposed to have dealings with one another.

You could die of thirst in that culture if you asked a drink of someone whose nationality was different from yours; and too bad if he—or she in this case—happened to be the only one around with a bucket and a rope long enough to draw water from such a deep well! The "rule" was that severe.

Or, in the case of the Canaanite woman, your child could be suffering horribly from some affliction, but you could only look on enviously at others getting healed by Jesus. You couldn't go to Him yourself, because both your nations didn't want to have dealings with one another.

But, as I said, the Canaanite woman was different. She wasn't going to let those manmade rules deny her of her miracle. She had faith in Jesus. She believed that He would bend the rules for her sake. She saw beyond His negative reply to His heart of love and compassion. The result? Jesus commended her for her great faith, and He granted her the miracle she had asked for.

---

[4] She was initially shocked at His asking her for a drink. But subsequently they had a long conversation together, and she ended up going back to her village to tell everyone about Him (*see John 4:7-30*).

CHAPTER 5

The Power of Different Thinking

DIFFERENT THINKING RAISES UP TRAILBLAZERS, HISTORY makers and world changers. Think of the exceptional thinkers and doers we have been talking about in this book—Elijah, Elisha, Daniel, Joshua, Abraham, David, Mary and Paul, to name just a few. Though these people have passed on a long time ago, the legacy of faith and excellence they left behind continues to inspire us to this day.

Independent thinkers in every age have been a potent force for good. They have stirred up the sleeping giant in many who were wasting their lives away and inspired them to make something of themselves. They have modeled for us what it means to have total trust in God. They have done the impossible with the help of God and, in so doing, have testified conclusively to His faithfulness and power. Through them, the glory of God has been revealed to all the world.

Different thinking is a quiet revolution that starts from within; it ignites the tiny spark of greatness inherent in each of us. It transforms us spiritually and mentally into giants and geniuses with the power to change our communities, nations, and even the world for the better. It spurs us on to reform unproductive systems and structures and to get rid of outdated, self-defeating customs, practices and regulations. Different thinking is contagious; it energizes us to achieve much more than we thought we could, and we soon become enthusiastic about getting others to think and do likewise too.

Different thinking starts with faith. The one thing that differentiates a different thinker from others is his absolute faith in God and himself. He fully believes that all things are possible when he teams up with God. Faith fuels the fire in him and gives him the tenacity to fight on and overcome the world. As it says in the Bible: "whatever is born of God overcomes the world. And this is the victory that has overcome the world—our faith" (*1 John 5:4, NKJV*).

Different thinking directs our destiny. This is why we can't afford to give up midway; there is too much at stake. No matter how much the enemy tries to stop you, you need to press on until you have achieved your purpose. When the devil sees that you are unstoppable, he will be the one to give up—because you are just too much work for him to handle!

After forty days of fasting and praying in the wilderness, Jesus was very hungry. It was then that the devil tried to trap Him: *You see all these stones around you? Turn them into bread! Eat and be filled!* But Jesus saw through his ruse and resisted the temptation to misuse His power. He stood firm on the Word: "It is written, 'Man shall not live on bread alone, but on every word that comes from the mouth of God'".

Then Satan took Jesus to the temple at Jerusalem and tempted Him to jump off its highest point, saying that God would surely come to His rescue. Again, Jesus quoted God's Word to refute him: "Do not put God to a foolish test." Finally came the big one—what the devil was really after:

> Next the devil took him to the peak of a very high mountain and showed him all the kingdoms of the world and their glory. "I will give it all to you," he said, "if you will kneel down and worship me."
>
> *Matthew 4:8-9, NLT*

Kneel down and worship me! I will give you all the kingdoms of the world and all their power and glory and riches. Forget about crucifixion; forget about why you came to earth; forget about saving mankind. Satan thought he had made Jesus an irresistible offer: everything the flesh could desire. But what was Jesus' response?

> "Get out of here, Satan," Jesus told him. "For the Scriptures say, 'You must worship the LORD your God and serve only him.'" Then the devil went away…
>
> *Matthew 4:10-11, NLT*

The enemy had to concede defeat. He gave up and left Jesus alone because he realized that he was wasting his time on a Man who was never going to submit to him—a Man who, having set His face like a flint (*Isaiah 50:7*), was unstoppable as He pressed on towards the cross ahead of Him.

Satan couldn't stand Jesus quoting God's Word at him,[5] because the Word of God is "living and powerful, and sharper than any two-edged sword… a discerner of the thoughts and intents of the heart" (*Hebrews 4:12, NKJV*). The deceiver of the world (*Revelation 12:9*) certainly wouldn't want his evil thoughts and intents to be discerned and exposed!

Like Jesus, we are going to face opposition from Satan as long as we are in this world. We are going to have to stand steadfast against temptations and tribulations of all kinds, and we will need the Word of God as our guide and mainstay. But we are not doing this alone; Christ is with us, and He is saying to us: "In the world you will have tribulation; but be of good cheer, I have overcome the world" (*John 16:33, NKJV*).

---

[5] Satan couldn't stand Jesus quoting God's Word *correctly and for the right purpose.* The devil himself quoted Scripture too (*see Matthew 4:6*), but he was misusing the text he quoted to further his own evil ends.

Be of good cheer. Because, as Christ overcame, so shall we. We are going to take new, untraveled paths. Life is going to be a wonderful ride, with never a dull moment. Like Jesus, we are going to be unstoppable; we are going to accomplish all that God has ordained for us to do. And what we have learnt in this book is going to help us achieve all this.

This book is meant, not just to encourage you to be a different thinker, but to be a different *doer* too; it is meant to inspire you to make a difference in the world in a positive way. And here I would like to sound a note of caution: keep in mind that, just as different thinking can be a vital force for good, it can also be a vicious force for evil. A disappointed or embittered different thinker is a dangerous person. He can become a powerful tool in the hands of the enemy.

If we are not careful, we can find ourselves misusing our power and influence, with disastrous consequences. To a certain extent, different thinking has a way of turning people into charismatic leaders—for good or ill. Think of all that humanity has suffered because certain very influential leaders manipulated their followers for their own selfish, destructive ends. Or, they saw a need for change but went about it the wrong way and created even more problems.

Different thinking is meant to benefit the world, not destroy it. My prayer is that you go forth and be the kind of different thinker the world needs: one who unites people, not sow discord; one who brings faith and hope, not fear or despair; one who brings light and life, not darkness or death.

May the Lord bless you and keep you. May the Lord make His face shine upon you. May the Lord be gracious to you. May the Lord lift up His countenance upon you. May the Lord give you peace. Shalom!